VOLLEYBALL

SKILLS *of the* GAME

Volleyball

Keith Nicholls

The Crowood Press

First published in 2001 by
The Crowood Press Ltd
Ramsbury, Marlborough
Wiltshire SN8 2HR

British Library Cataloguing-in-Publication Data
A catalogue record for this book is available from the British
Library.

ISBN 1 86126 441 0

Acknowledgements
Fig 3 was supplied by Nevobo and Figs 127, 128 and 130 by Keith
Nicholls; all other photographs by Barbara Totterdell.

Line drawings by Annette Findlay and Vanetta Joffe.

Typefaces used: Galliard (main text); Franklin Gothic Heavy
(chapter headings); Univers Condensed (labels).

Typeset and designed by
D & N Publishing
Baydon, Marlborough, Wiltshire

Printed and bound in Great Britain by JW Arrowsmith, Bristol.

Contents

Introduction

ORIGINS

One of the most popular events at the Sydney Olympic Games with spectators at the competition and watching on TV around the world, was that of volleyball both on the beach and indoors. The transformation of Sydney's world famous Bondi Beach into the Olympic Beach Volleyball Arena brought the vibrancy of volleyball to the attention of millions. From a game invented purely as a leisurely recreation it has now become, after basketball, the world's most played game. A survey of the number of players registered with each national governing body in the Olympic sports has shown that basketball and volleyball both have over 70 million competitive players around the world. Football, normally considered the most popular sport, has less than half this total.

William Morgan, who was Director of Recreation at Holyoke YMCA in Massachusetts, invented the game in 1895. During the two World Wars, American servicemen spread the game around the world and it soon became established in Europe and Asia. Gradually the game developed past the stage of being just a recreation into a fully competitive sport played at international level. The biggest breakthrough came in 1964 when volleyball became the first Olympic team sport for men and women. The tremendous impact, made by the Japanese ladies' team in particular, led to an explosion of interest around the world. Suddenly the game became a battle between Eastern Europe and the rest of the world. Governments invested heavily in developing the sport in the search for international success. By the mid-1980s the USA, Republic of China, Cuba and the Soviet Union had become the dominant countries. In response countries such as Italy, Holland and Germany developed strong semi-professional leagues and their national teams entered into full-time training. The establishment of World Cups and Leagues for the top national teams has followed. Unlike sports such as football, the main competitive emphasis in volleyball is on matches between national teams rather than clubs. As a result, many countries keep their teams together almost full time and their players do not play in club-based competition at all.

This regular international competition has meant that spectators all around the world have had the chance to see volleyball played at its best. They have marvelled at the speed and agility, the power, the subtlety and the sportsmanship that

---

Some Interesting Facts

- Played competitively by over 70 million people worldwide
- An Olympic sport since 1964 for men and women
- Beach volleyball became an Olympic sport in Atlanta in 1996
- Twice as many people play competitive volleyball as play football

have been displayed. Millions of people have, as a result, been encouraged to go out and improve their own play or to take up the game.

A SPORT FOR ALL

A great feature of volleyball is its adaptability – it can be played by all ages in sports halls and gymnasiums, in parks, playgrounds and on the beach. Versions of the game have been developed for two, three and four players, for younger players, and sitting volleyball for disabled players.

The fire services around the world have adopted volleyball as their major game as it can be played in station yards as part of the physical training programme. Each year there is a European Fire Service Championship as well as European Championships for the Armed Forces and the police.

VARIATIONS

Mini-Volleyball

Mini-volleyball is a specially developed version of the game to take into account both the smaller hands of younger players and the need for a lower net. Although primarily a game for nine- to thirteen-year-olds, there is no reason why other age groups cannot learn to play.

The net height for this age group is 2.10m, which will still enable them to smash and serve with correct technique and allow the back-court skills to develop. The court is reduced in size to 9m long and 5m wide. On this smaller court there are only three players on each side. The ball is smaller, with a 62cm diameter instead of the normal 65–67cm.

Fig 1   Outdoor tournaments are enjoyed by hundreds of players and teams.

Outdoor Volleyball

Across the world vast outdoor tournaments attract hundreds of teams. Camping in adjoining fields, enthusiasts can play from dawn to dusk. The largest European tournaments attract the top club sides as well as touring sides from other parts of the world. In Britain there are three major summer tournaments each with over two hundred teams taking part in each event every year.

At these tournaments there are leagues for top teams, average club sides, novices, juniors and 'masters' in both sexes. Wind, rain or sunshine is no obstacle to play. There is a wonderful social atmosphere and players often combine from several clubs just for a particular tournament.

Park Volley

The FIVB have developed Park Volley, which is played by two teams of four on a court 14m × 7m. It is an ideal recreational form of volleyball although players who are more competent as well can enjoy it. The net height is reduced to 2.15m for players up to 12 years, and at 13 years of age the height for boys is raised to 2m 30cm and for girls to 2m 24cm. Over 18, it is recommended that the standard net heights and court size be used. Portable net systems are available that can be set up in parks or gardens to play Park Volley.

Beach Volleyball

On beaches throughout the world, volleyball is a game for relaxation as well as competition. Holidaymakers can knock a plastic beach ball back and forth between bouts of sunbathing and swimming.

For the serious player there are beach competitions. In California particularly, beach volleyball is a big spectator event attracting

Fig 2   Beach Volleyball – an Olympic sport that attracts huge crowds on beaches around the world.

thousands. Beach volleyball is a full Olympic sport and there is annual Grand Prix tour playing not just on beaches but also on specially prepared courts in major inland cities around the world with prize money of $5 million.

Although there are six-a-side competitions, beach volleyball is usually played with two players per side. Mixed teams usually play four-a-side with special rules to allow more equal competition between the male and female players on each side. The court for beach volleyball is slightly smaller than normal at 16m long by 8m wide to take into account the reduced number of players.

Sitting and Standing Volleyball

One of my most enduring memories in volleyball is playing with a club team against the British Standing Volleyball team preparing to compete in an international tournament. The team had three players with artificial legs and one with only one leg. Needless to say, my team felt that we should slow our game down and make allowances for their handicaps. It took less than half a set for them to make the point quite clearly that if we did not want to suffer a very quick defeat we had better play our normal game! The ability of their players to adapt their style of play to suit their strengths was quite enlightening.

Sitting volleyball has been developed for those with mobility problems and is played in the ParaOlympics. The net is obviously lower and the court slightly smaller but the differences end there. The players use their hands to move their bodies around the court so quickly that few balls land without some form of contact.

Masters' Volleyball

Age is no barrier in volleyball. In fact, many international players continue until their late thirties, as experience and skill acquired over a long period are essential to the game. In recent years a flourishing masters circuit has been established in Europe, with classes for teams of players over forty, fifty and sixty years old, and aggregate age teams. In Finland the annual President's Cup, instituted by a former President of Finland, attracts hundreds of teams from all over Europe.

Fig 3   Sitting volleyball is a popular game with Olympic and World championships.

CHAPTER 1
Getting Started

RULES

There are very few lines on a volleyball court and only twenty-eight rules that govern how volleyball is played; this makes volleyball, relative to other team games, quite easy to understand.

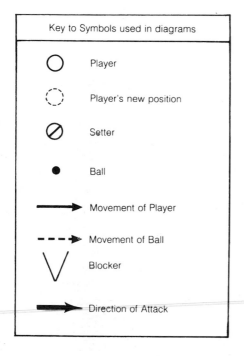

Key to Symbols used in diagrams

○   Player

◌   Player's new position

⊘   Setter

●   Ball

⟶   Movement of Player

--→   Movement of Ball

V   Blocker

⟶   Direction of Attack

The Court

The court is 18m long and 9m wide. Separating the court into 9m squares is the net, which is 1m in depth and varies in height depending on age or sex. For women the height is 2.24m and for men the height is raised to 2.43m. At younger age levels, the net height can be reduced. The International Volleyball Federation (FIVB) recommend a height of 2.15m for boys and girls aged 9–12 years, rising to 2.30m for boys up to 17 years. Girls adopt the standard women's height of 2.24m at 13 years.

During the game, all boundary lines count as part of the court, and any ball landing on the line is considered 'in court'. In each court there is an 'attack line' that is 3m from the net. In the attack zone, there are restrictions on how the backcourt players may play the ball.

There is no designated serving area on the back line as the server may position themselves anywhere in the 9m zone between the two sidelines. If the player contacts the baseline or the area in the court during the service before or whilst the ball is struck, the serve is illegal.

Officials

There are two officials in volleyball; they are called the first and second referees and have different powers and functions during the game. The first referee is in overall charge of the game and is positioned on a stand just off court in line with the net, so that he or she can see along the top of the net and both halves of the court.

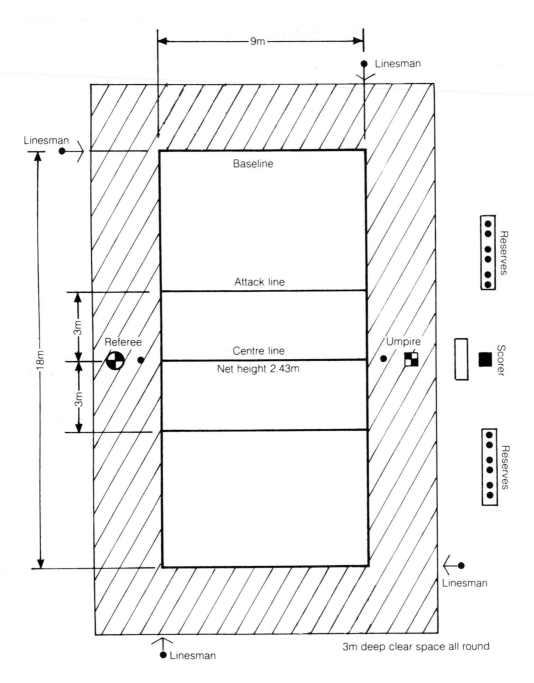

Fig 4   The volleyball court. The height of the net is 2.24m for women and 2.43m for men.

This referee decides whether the ball has been played legally and when to award a point. In addition, this referee is solely responsible for calling touches at the top of the net and for disciplining players.

On the opposite side of the court, but not on a stand, is the second referee. This referee controls substitutions, time-outs, checks players' rotations, net offences below the top of the net, and oversees the scoring table and official warm-up.

Both teams have a team bench on the same side of the court as the second referee, and the scorer's table is positioned between the two teams. Only coaches and players on the team sheet may sit on the team bench. The coach may coach the players from the side of the court provided that he or she remains in the area between the attack line and the baseline without interfering with play. Players waiting to go on court should wait on the bench or in the special area at the end of the court.

To help the officials determine whether balls land in or out of court there are either two or four line judges. The second referee will allocate the line judges responsibility for one or two lines and they signal both when the ball lands in court and out of court. If a player touches the ball on its way out of court they signal this as well.

The net extends over the sidelines and a white band is attached to the net above the sideline to indicate the court boundary. Attached to this band are flexible 'antennae' that are red and white and extend above the court. Their purpose is to identify balls crossing the net outside the boundary lines, and they may not be contacted during play by the ball or players.

The Players

Each team is allowed up to twelve players in their squad but only six of these may play on

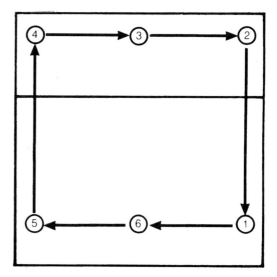

Fig 5   The numbering system and direction of rotation.

court at a time. The other players act as substitutes. The six players on court will be assigned positions as shown in Fig 5. The six court positions are numbered in an anti-clockwise direction starting with the back right position. Players in Positions 2, 3 and 4 are known as the frontcourt players and 1, 6 and 5 as the backcourt players.

Every player will play in six positions (except the libero player – *see* next page) during a game. When a side serves the ball into play and wins the rally, it wins a point. If they lose the rally their opponents score a point and the right to serve passes to the other side. The new serving side rotates one place clockwise so that the player previously in Position 2 now serves the ball from Position 1. All the other players will also be playing in their next court position. The original idea of this rule was to avoid players becoming solely attackers or defenders. Over the years this specialization has developed but the rotation rule does add tremendous variety to the game.

The Libero Player

Only six players are allowed on court at any time. Players may be substituted on and off court during a set. One player known as the libero only plays in the backcourt of the game, that is, in Positions 1, 6 and 5. He is not able to serve the ball, block, attempt to block the ball or make an attack hit if the ball is entirely higher than the top of the net at the point of contact. The libero player may not use the overhead pass to play the ball for a frontcourt player to attack. The role of the libero is primarily as a defensive backcourt specialist. To help the referees distinguish the libero from the other players they wear a different-coloured shirt. Unlike other players the libero may come onto court to replace another player before the rally starts without having to ask permission from the second referee. He can come off court at the end of any rally but if his team has rotated so that he would have to move to the frontcourt, he must come off and be replaced by the original player in that position.

Any player on court may be substituted once in each set with a player from the team bench. Once a player on court has been substituted he can only go back on court during that set for his replacement. This can only happen once in each set with this pair of players. Each time a player comes off court, this counts as one substitution; a maximum of six substitutions is allowed in each set. This means that coaches can have six completely new players on court or a combination of the original line-up and substitutes.

The coach or court captain can substitute players at the end of rallies by asking the second referee. He will then ensure that the team has not used all their substitutions, that the player going on court is eligible and that the scorer has recorded the numbers of the players involved.

Time-Outs

Each team is allowed two time-outs per set and they last a maximum of thirty seconds. The team coach or captain on court wanting the time-out must ask the second referee as soon as the rally ends. During the time-out the players must leave the court area and join the coach and substitutes at the bench. In International matches there are two additional compulsory time outs each set – to allow for advertising breaks on television!

Scoring

Matches are the best of three or five sets with the first two or three sets being played until one team reaches a minimum of 25 points with a two point advantage. If the score reaches 24:24 play continues until one team has a two point advantage. In the deciding set, play continues until one team has a minimum of 15 points and a two point advantage.

Points are scored on every rally. Rallies come to an end when:

- A team grounds the ball in its opponents' court;
- A team fails to return the ball legally across the net within a maximum of three touches of the ball;
- A player plays the ball illegally, touches the net or crosses into the opponents' court;
- Players are out of their rotational order;
- The first referee awards a point against a player or team for misconduct.

The two teams toss for service or choice of ends at the start of the match and before the start of a deciding set. In this set the teams change ends when the leading team scores eight points. The interval between sets is three minutes.

Three Touch Volleyball

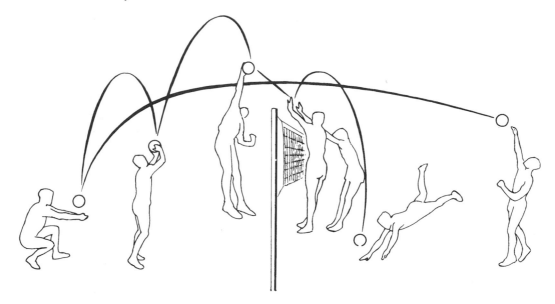

Fig 6   The pattern of play in volleyball.

The normal pattern of play is shown in Fig 6. Teams aim to use the three permitted touches to make the best attack possible. Although there are occasions when playing the ball across the net on the first or second touch can be effective or necessary, generally speaking 'three touch volleyball' is best.

The serve is received on the outstretched forearms with a 'dig pass' and this is often referred to as the 'first pass'. A player with the specialist role of 'setter' will use a 'volley pass' to 'set up' the attack for one of the players to hit the ball across into the opponents' court. The technique used for most attacks is the 'smash' which involves jumping as high as possible and hitting the ball down into the opponents' court. On the other side of the net, frontcourt players will try to 'block' the ball by jumping up and placing a wall of hands into the path of the ball. Sometimes the ball will be played just over the block or it may rebound off it and a backcourt player will have to 'dive' to play the ball.

When the block touches the ball a unique situation is created in the game. Normally no player may touch the ball twice in succession on his side of the net. If, however, he blocks the ball he may play the ball again without another player touching it in between. A touch of the ball by blocking does not count as one of the three touches for the team. The reason for this is to enable teams to make a good attack using the three-touch pattern of dig–set–smash.

Each of the techniques in the game is affected by the rules in terms of movements that are allowed. For the beginner it will be rather frustrating at first to find the game being stopped for handling faults. As the techniques become more reliable this will occur much less frequently.

Equipment

Very little equipment is needed to get started in volleyball, but it is most important to see that the equipment you buy is both safe and suitable. A lot of equipment that is offered may seem attractive in price but may be very uncomfortable to play with. All governing bodies for the sport operate an approval scheme and you are strongly advised to consult them or a specialist volleyball retailer before making a purchase.

Posts

Posts are the only expensive item of equipment but for safety reasons alone must be chosen with care.

The first and most important point is that posts supported by weights or tensioned by wires to the floor or walls are illegal and dangerous. Teachers, coaches and players should refuse to use them. Weighted posts can be brought down by contact with the net; players can trip over the weights during play or run into the guy wires and receive serious injuries.

Posts should be screwed to the floor or fitted into floor sockets that are positioned between 0.5m and 1m from the sideline. The base of the posts should not project forward as players could trip over them. The governing bodies or volleyball specialists will advise on approved posts.

The most important thing about the ball is that it should be made with a leather surface and that it should be the correct weight. A ball that is too heavy can damage the fingers and wrists during play.

For the purposes of teaching, a lightweight smooth plastic or dense foam ball can be used as these will not cause injury. Materials such as rubber, nylon or vinyl are very unsuitable – balls made of these materials should never be used.

When buying a ball you should decide whether it is for match play or training. Match play balls are of two categories, international and league standard. Balls approved for international play will have the FIVB stamp on them. Normally if a ball is approved for league or match play it will carry the approval stamp of the national associations, but some approved balls do not. A list of all approved balls can be obtained from the national associations. The difference in quality between the two grades of ball is mainly in the softness of the leather covering.

All match play balls are laceless and made with a rubber core covered with leather panels. The better balls normally have softer leather and a free-floating bladder that cushions the ball on impact. A special thin needle inflator must be used with this type of ball and the valve should be flush fitting with the surface.

Training balls will not be approved by the governing bodies but are very suitable for teaching or training when many balls are needed. When choosing a training ball it is best to check with one of the specialist volleyball retailers as they can give advice on what is currently available. What you should look for is a ball of the correct size and weight which is round and will retain its shape for a long time. The leather will not be of such good quality as that used for the match play balls and may seem at first to be unyielding. Many of these balls will soften with use and this is where the specialist retailer can give good advice. Also, check the valve to see that it is as flush fitting as possible. On many cheap balls, there is a circular lump around the valve and these should be avoided as the flight path of the ball, particularly when served, will be affected.

Check that the surface of the ball is natural leather not synthetic, Clarino or

PVC leather. These leather substitutes are only suitable for balls used in outdoor tournaments or beach volleyball where natural leather will absorb moisture. They are however harder on the arms and tend to be slippery when damp. They are not approved for indoor matches and are not suitable for teaching.

New balls are now on the market to help introduce the game to younger players. Smaller balls – mini-volleyballs – are now available for younger players and are widely used in schools and mini-volley competitions. The circumference of these balls – 62cm as opposed to 65–67cm for the normal ball – suits the smaller hands of the younger player and helps develop good handling techniques. Also available are larger balls – 25 per cent larger – that move more slowly through the air giving novice players more time to move into position.

Net

As with balls, there are match play and practice nets with considerable variations in price. A good match play net should last a couple of seasons without getting a hole in it, whereas practice nets are only good enough for one season. The governing bodies operate an approval scheme that will guarantee that the net conforms to the rules with regard to dimensions, construction and materials.

The net must be 9.5m long and 1m in depth with a 10cm mesh. To help get even tension of the mesh, many nets have wooden slats at the ends that are then tied to the posts fully stretching the net horizontally. During play a ball can, in some circumstances, be played after rebounding from the net so it needs good overall tension.

Cheaper practice nets are suitable for class teaching and outdoor recreational play but generally are not a good buy as they have to be replaced quickly and the ball will not rebound off them. A good buy for schools is a long teaching net that will fit the length of the sports hall. This can then be divided into smaller courts by hanging coloured bands at intervals.

Net Antennae

The net is wider than the court and a white vertical marker is fitted to the net directly above each of the sidelines. Into this marker is fitted a fibreglass antennae that projects 80cm above the net. When a ball touches the aerial during play or passes across the net outside the aerial a fault occurs. Antennae can be made in one or two pieces – experience shows that the one piece lasts much longer.

Individual Kit

A player needs very little personal kit for volleyball, but should take care to select kit designed for volleyball and not football, basketball, squash and so on. The needs of every sport are different and in order to participate to the best of your ability you should not be restricted by kit of poor design. Kit designed for volleyball is available and most volleyball teams will support the view that the demands of the game are such that it is necessary.

Clothing

Shirts need a generous cut under the arms. When smashing the ball you need to be able to stretch your arms freely without pulling your shirt out or feeling restricted. When diving and sliding on the floor it should not pull around the neck. The choice of long or short sleeves is a personal one. Many players prefer the freedom of short sleeves while others like the extra protection when defending in backcourt. Shorts should allow free range of movement from the low position in backcourt to the run-up for a smash and vice versa.

Shoes

When playing, you will be changing quickly from one action to another – one moment jumping to smash, the next to block, then turning to play a ball and so on. Your feet will take a lot of pounding in the course of a match and a properly designed pair of shoes is essential, not only to avoid injury but to enable you to perform to your full potential.

Shoes should have flexible soles to enable you to take off and land correctly for the smash and block. They need a good grip to push off and stop quickly in defence while still allowing you to turn and pivot. A lot of research has taken place into the demands of volleyball on feet and there are a number of specialist shoes on the market designed to cover all these aspects; again a specialist retailer can give you good advice.

Ball

If you want to get the most out of volleyball then you need your own ball. It is not necessary to buy a full international match ball, a good training ball will suffice.

With your own ball you can practise the volley, dig or smash against a wall at home or school, and play a game in the garden or park or on the beach with friends or family. Later in the book you will find practices you can try with your own ball.

CHAPTER 2

Attacking Skills

In this chapter, you will learn about the three attacking skills, serving, the volley pass and the smash. In common with other team games, volleyball consists of two elements, attack and defence, but unlike other games every player is required to master all the skills in both elements.

If we look at a typical rally, we can see the following pattern: serve – receive of serve – volley pass – smash – block – backcourt defensive pass – set pass, and so on. The main attacking skills are the serve, the volley pass and the smash. A good serve will score a point directly or put the opposition under pressure, and an accurate and well-placed pass is essential to set up the smash.

THE SERVE

The Role of the Serve in Volleyball

The serve puts the ball in play and creates a scoring opportunity for both teams. A team only requires twenty-five points to win the set, just fifteen in the deciding set. There is nothing more morale boosting for a team than to see the opposing server put the ball out of court or into the net giving them an uncontested point. When the match is very close or near the end of a set, this is a real bonus!

There is a real dilemma facing the server. The receiving side makes the first attack and statistically has a 60 per cent chance of success. If the ball is served just to ensure it goes into play then it is making it very easy for the opponents to set up an attack and win the point. If the server goes for the ace, the risk of an error increases and the point is more likely to be given away. Serving is, therefore, a critical skill to develop, but surprisingly one which many coaches and players do not give enough attention to.

What is the Bottom Line?

The player, coach and team are looking for:

- Reliability
- Accuracy
- Effectiveness

Each player must develop a serve that is reliable, that can be played repeatedly with a low error rate. Once that consistency has been developed they must be able to serve the ball to all points of the court and make it as difficult as possible to receive. Serving is the only skill in the game where the player has total control, he/she does not have to play a moving ball or avoid an opponent. If the player can't get the ball into court every time, aimed at the most tactically effective position and as difficult as possible for the opponent to play then the advantage is handed back to the other team.

The quickest way to improve a team's performance is by maximizing the effectiveness of each player's serve.

THE TYPES OF SERVE

Four main types of serve have evolved over the years reflecting changes in the rules, tactics and the ball itself: underarm, overhead, floating and jump serves. Each has its advantages and disadvantages.

THE UNDERARM SERVE
(Figs 7–8)

This is the easiest and most reliable method of serving. Relying on co-ordination rather than strength, this serve is the perfect choice for the novice player. Every player should be able to achieve a high standard of reliability with this serve.

The serve can be broken down into four stages: the stance, positioning the ball, the swing and making contact.

Stance

Face the direction the ball is to go with the feet pointing at the target player or point on court. If right-handed, the left foot should be forward and the reverse for left-handers.

To achieve the maximum accuracy it is important to avoid any rotation of the hips and shoulders. So, ensure that the feet, hips and shoulders point towards the target right at the start. The knees should be slightly bent, and to start with keep the weight over the front foot.

Positioning the Ball

The key to successful striking of the ball is two straight arms (Fig 7). Hold the ball in the hand just in front of the hips, directly in the path of the striking arm that will swing down outside the hips. Keep the striking arm straight and place it directly behind the ball.

Fig 7 The basic stance for the underarm serve, with the ball held directly in the path of the hitting arm.

Adopting this position ensures that the ball is struck directly in line with the target.

Swing

The action of hitting the ball must be smooth, and by transferring the body weight in line with the arm swing, very little strength is needed. As the hitting arm is swung back behind the shoulder, the body weight is moved onto the back foot with a rocking action.

Making Contact

With the weight on the back foot and the hitting arm kept straight and behind the body directly in line with the ball, start the serve.

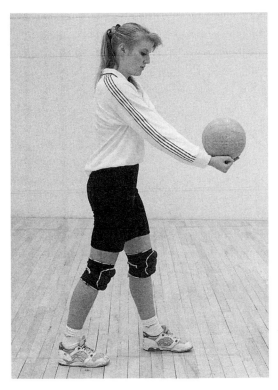

Fig 8 The ball is hit with the heel of the hand or closed fist.

Swing the arm forwards like a pendulum close to the hips as the weight is transferred onto the front foot. Make contact with the ball using the heel of the hand or the closed fist, not the palm (Fig 8).

It is important that after contacting the ball the swing is continued in the direction of

---

Underarm Serve – Tips

- Face direction of serve
- Point feet, hips, shoulders toward target
- Hold ball in path of striking arm
- Swing hitting arm like a pendulum to contact ball
- Hit ball with heel of hand or closed fist
- Transfer your body weight after the ball

---

the target. At the same time, it is helpful to continue the body-weight transfer by stepping after the ball. Not only will this give extra power; it will also get you moving forward on court and into your defensive position.

You cannot hit the ball directly out of the hand so make sure you pull it away just before you make contact. The ball should not be thrown up into the air, as this will make it more difficult to time the contact.

OVERHEAD SERVE (Figs 9–11)

The overhead serve is the most widely used in the game. Small variations of the basic technique enable the server to alter the flight of the ball by adding spin or 'floating' the ball. The ball will 'float', that is swerve or dip without warning, when it is hit without spin and hard enough to achieve a critical speed that will cause the air flow and pressures around the ball to affect its movement. This unpredictability causes problems for the receiver.

Strike the ball at or near net height to give the ball a flatter trajectory across the net reducing the time available to the receiver.

Stance

Again aim the feet and body at the target player or area with the right foot half a pace back – left foot for a left-hander. It is very important that from the start of the serve the ball is positioned in front of the hitting shoulder (Fig 9). This will ensure not only good contact but also maximum power.

This serve does require more strength than the underarm and it is helpful to step into the serve to add the effect of transferring the momentum of the body. So start with the weight on the back foot (Fig 10) with the feet, hips and shoulders angled

Fig 9 For the overhead serve the ball is held directly in front of the hitting arm just above shoulder height.

Fig 10 The weight starts on the back foot with the feet pointing in the direction of the serve.

towards the target. The starting position behind the baseline should allow for any forward movement to the ball.

The Toss

This is the point where most errors occur. Throw the ball vertically so that it will drop in front of the hitting shoulder. If there is to be a step into playing the ball, throw it further forward.

Start by extending the non-striking arm in front of the opposite shoulder with the ball in the palm of the hand. Place the striking hand behind the ball. This position establishes the correct relationship between the ball and the player. When contacted, the ball should be in front of the player and the hitting shoulder. If the ball is too close to the player or out of line with the shoulder, the accuracy and reliability of the serve is reduced.

The hitting arm is withdrawn keeping the elbow higher than the shoulder so that the final contact will be as high as possible (Fig 11). As this happens the ball is tossed upwards and forwards. The distance forwards depends on whether the player is just stepping into the ball or adding an additional stride.

An accurate toss is essential and this is made easier if it starts at shoulder height. When the hand drops below this height the path of the hand before release can cause problems with accuracy. The height of the toss

Fig 11   Just before the ball is tossed up the hitting arm is pulled back.

Overhead Serve – Tips

- Face direction of serve
- Point feet, hips, shoulders toward target
- Step into serve for added power
- Toss ball in front of hitting shoulder
- Withdraw hitting arm keeping elbow high
- Rotate striking arm forwards and upwards
- Make contact as high as possible just in front of the shoulder
- Hit ball with open hand
- Follow through and move into backcourt defensive position
- Transfer your body weight after the ball

varies with the player and the timing of the serve but is usually between 50cm and 150cm.

Making Contact

Pulling the hitting arm back induces a rotation of the shoulders and upper body and transfers the body weight onto the rear foot. The power for the serve is generated from this position. Step forward towards the dropping ball and rotate the body and hitting arm forwards and upwards. The elbow should remain in a high position and lead the hand. A high point of contact is essential not only for the serve to clear the net but to give the receiver less time to view the path of the ball.

Make sure that at the point of contact the ball is directly in front of the shoulder, the arm is straight and the hips and shoulders have rotated into alignment.

Contact the ball with the open hand. For a normal overhead serve, the arm follows the ball and the transfer of body weight continues into the next stride onto court.

This basic technique can be used to deliver a tactically placed ball playing on a positional or player weakness.

As mentioned earlier, the basic technique can be adapted to produce a floating or topspin serve.

FLOATING SERVE

The receiver will try to predict the best place to play the ball from cues such as previous serves, the position of the server or the type of serve. A good floating serve is hard to hit but will be very difficult for the receiver to predict. The laws of aerodynamics affect the flight of a ball hit without spin and it can therefore swerve or dip unpredictably towards the end of its flight. The receiver is then forced to make last-minute adjustments to their court or body position and this can adversely affect the quality of their pass.

Ensure that the ball is hit without spin, otherwise the ball will not float.

The toss will normally be low so that there is less chance of spin being induced during the toss and the server can accurately time the hit. Contact with the ball must be firm. Keep the hand rigid throughout the contact phase, driving into the ball but then stopping all movement sharply.

TOPSPIN SERVE

The topspin serve is harder and faster than other overhead serves. It also dips sharply at the end, forcing the receiver to get low to get under the ball. Whereas in the basic overhead serve and the floating serve the body movements are essentially parallel to the floor to drive the ball forward, to produce spin a circular body movement must be created. The toss is higher than other overhead serves and ideally should give the ball a forward spin.

JUMP SERVE

One of the most exciting technical developments in volleyball in recent years has been the emergence of the jump serve. The start of a rally with a jump serve is dramatic; the ball is hit with considerable force in a flat trajectory across the net putting receivers under great pressure.

The two main advantages of this serve are speed and trajectory. As the player runs and jumps into the serving action, he/she is able to use a larger range of motion, create more force and achieve greater speed. The contact point is often well above the floor so the trajectory of the ball is flatter. These two factors together give the receiver a lot less time to get into the right court and body position to play the ball.

However, a much higher error rate and lower levels of accuracy offset these advantages. With the introduction of rally point scoring, the importance of reliability has increased and the use of this serve needs to be carefully assessed on an individual and situational basis.

Starting about 3m from the baseline, toss the ball forward and upwards into a position where it reaches its highest point approximately 50cm behind the baseline. As with all serves, an accurate toss is vital for a successful jump serve. The height of the toss is very individual and is linked to the speed of the approach and the height of the jump.

Throwing the ball up and moving forward are simultaneous and most players find it easier to toss the ball with one hand. After stepping forward lower the hand holding the ball

Fig 12 Jump serve – the toss.

Fig 13 Jump serve – the first step.

Fig 14 Jump serve – during the approach swing the arms back behind the body.

– right for right-handed players and vice-versa. As your right arm moves upward to release the ball, the left arm moves forward with the next step (Fig 12). When tossing the ball, release it from the fingertips imparting topspin. Topspin will help with the final contact stage of the serve. The first step (Fig 13) following the toss is the key to the success of the serve as it determines the timing. There must be an acceleration forward culminating in a forceful take-off similar to that used for the smash.

During the approach, swing the arms back behind the body (Fig 14). As your feet are planted for take-off, swing the arms forwards and upwards (Fig 15).

Bend the hitting arm keeping the elbow high. If you have made a strong take-off, your back will arch, creating a strong position to commence the serve (Fig 16). By contracting the stomach muscles and bringing the upper body forward, the arm can swing forcefully forwards to contact the ball. At this point, the ball should be above net height and dropping in front of your hitting shoulder. The hand should contact the ball below its midpoint and the palm rotated upwards and forwards to add topspin.

After hitting the ball, the player prepares for landing and moving into his/her back-court defensive position. Players with good technique and a high jump will be able to

take off behind the baseline and hit the ball several feet inside the court. This is legal and will increase the effectiveness of the serve. However, it should not be at the expense of reliability.

ABOVE LEFT: Fig 15 Jump serve – as the feet are planted for take-off the arms are swung forward.

ABOVE: Fig 16 Jump serve – the back arches with the hitting arm bent ready to begin the hitting action.

Jump Serve – Tips

- Start about 3m behind baseline
- Toss ball upwards to reach its high point just behind the baseline
- Give the ball forward spin
- During the approach, swing the arms back to aid take-off
- After take-off, pull the hitting arm back with elbow high

- Contract the stomach muscles and pull the shoulders
- Rotate striking arm forwards and upwards
- Make contact as high as possible just below the middle
- Hit ball with palm and rotate upwards and forwards to add spin
- Follow through and move into backcourt defensive position

Serving: Ten Keys to Success

1. **Focus and prepare well**
   As you walk back to serve, compose yourself, identify your target, and assume the correct body and court position before making eye contact with the referee.

2. **Be consistent**
   Establish a routine and keep to it.

3. **Establish the lines – ball and arm, ball and target**
   Check the position of the ball before the toss with the hitting arm; line up the ball and body with the target.

4. **Check the feet**
   The feet should be in line with the target.

5. **Build up the momentum**
   Give yourself room to move into the ball and transfer your body weight through it.

6. **Control the toss**
   Everything depends on an accurately placed toss bringing the ball directly into line with the arm and hand.

7. **Aim high**
   Reach up to the ball to ensure that you contact it as near or above net height as possible.

8. **Hit in front**
   Keep the ball in front of you in line with your shoulder for maximum power and accuracy.

9. **Make that contact**
   Ensure that you make a firm contact with the ball using the closed fist or open hand depending on the type of serve.

10. **Hit through the ball**
    Always follow through with the hand and body weight so that the serve is at maximum power.

THE VOLLEY PASS

The volley is the most accurate way of passing the ball and is used to set up the final attack. It is unlike any other sports technique where the ball is played with the hands because the rules do not allow you to catch, hold or throw the ball. However, the volley is not as difficult to master as it may seem.

The ball is played on the fingers of both hands above the head. Almost immediately after contact is made the arms and fingers extend to direct the ball towards its target. When you look at a good player they seem to play the ball smoothly with little effort.

A successful volley requires good preparation and anticipation. Anticipate the point on court where the ball will drop into the hands just in front of and above the forehead. Move quickly into position well before the ball arrives with the hands in the ready position. This enables final adjustments to the court, body and hand position to be made in good time.

It is important to be in a balanced and stationary position before playing the ball. Place your legs shoulder-width apart, slightly flexed with the right foot just in front of the left. Normally the ball will be coming from a different direction from the one you need to play it to so you must position yourself carefully. Move your feet, hips and shoulders round to face the direction you want to pass the ball.

Raise your arms as early as possible with the elbows at shoulder height and at an angle of 45 degrees to the chest. Spread the fingers of both hands wide with the palms towards each other.

Fig 17 Jump serve. Contact with the ball is directly in front of the hitting shoulder at the highest part the player can reach.

ABOVE: Fig 19   The fingers spread around the ball forming a cup shape.

BELOW: Fig 20   The ball must be played in the 'mid-line' of the body from a well-balanced position.

Fig 18   In the volley pass the hands are placed just above and in front of the forehead. The ball enters the cupped hands and contacts the finger lengths. The palms do not come into contact with the ball.

Cock the wrists back with the thumbs pointing back towards the face (Fig 18). This position forms a cup shape for the ball to drop into (Fig 19). It is helpful if you work with a partner to set this position up. Hold a ball firmly in the hands so that it rests on the forehead. Move the hands forward and upward 10–15cm and ask your partner to take the ball out of your hands. Keep the hands still and this is the correct position and shape to receive the ball.

Play the ball in the mid-line of the body so that the arm and body movement moves directly through the ball (Fig 20). It is important to keep the fingers relaxed, as you want to be able to let the ball enter the hands and not bounce out. As the ball touches the fingers, smoothly extend the arms from the shoulders upwards and forwards in the direction you

Fig 21 The ball is played just above and in front of the forehead, extend the legs off the back foot upwards and forwards right through contact with the ball.

want to pass (Fig 21). Resist the temptation to strike or bat the ball but wait for it to come into the hands. The ball does not touch the palm only the finger lengths. The thumbs stop the ball dropping down or coming through towards the head. The other fingers stop lateral movement of the ball.

As the arms extend, transfer the body weight from the back foot forwards and through the ball. This ensures that there is a direct line of force through the body and ball towards the target.

Although you are playing the ball to another player do not aim directly at them. Play the ball to a height of at least 5m so that it will drop in front of them. Remember height equals time and the more time the receiver has, the greater their chance of a successful play.

The Volley Pass: Ten Keys to Success

1. **Arrive early**
   Get to the point where you will contact the ball as early as possible to give yourself as much time as possible to adjust to the flight and the direction you wish to play.

2. **Keep balanced**
   As you move towards the ball, use short steps rather than long ones to keep yourself balanced.

3. **Play ball above and in front of forehead**
   Bend the legs to get below the ball and extend upwards and forwards as you play.

4. **Keep the ball in the midline**
   Play the ball in the centre of the body for maximum control and accuracy.

5. **Firm base**
   Adopt a firm base with the legs shoulder-width apart, right foot just ahead of the left.

6. **Shape of hands**
   Make a cup shape with the fingers to get maximum control of the ball.

7. **Elbows out**
   Form a 90-degree angle at the forefingers with the elbows.

8. **Stretch from the elbows**
   When the ball enters the hands, stretch the arms from the elbows upwards and forwards.

9. **Smooth release of ball & hand touch**
   Keep the fingers relaxed, make the contact and release movement smooth.

10. **Point thumbs after ball**
    Play through the ball by pointing the thumbs after the flight of the ball.

Training Practices

1. Place ball on ground, put hands around ball in correct position and lift ball above head. Throw ball gently up into the air from this position, catch and repeat.
2. In pairs; catch and throw, making sure ball is caught and thrown from above and in front of the head. Gradually cut down contact time until ball is volleyed and not thrown.
3. In pairs 4m apart; volley to each other and volley the ball 2m high above the head before returning it (Fig 22).

Fig 22

4. In pairs with two balls; one player feeds with underarm throw for partner to volley back. Make sure the ball is thrown high, about 5m. As the first ball is being played, throw the second. Keep both balls in play with a good rhythm.
5. In pairs 3m apart; one player feeds, the other volleys back then moves 3m to the side to play the ball a second time and so on (Fig 23).
6. Three players play the ball around a square. One player has to play two corners by moving across the diagonal. Make sure players move to face direction ball is to go before playing the ball (Fig 24).
7. In two lines 3m apart; pass and follow exercise. Try to keep path of the ball directly over one of the lines on the court (Fig 25).
8. In threes; the player in the centre returns ball to outside player then turns 180 degrees to face the other player. The two outside players play a short ball to the centre and a long ball to each other (Fig 26).

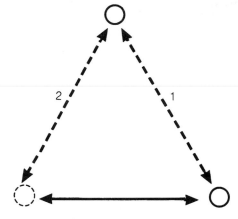

Fig 23

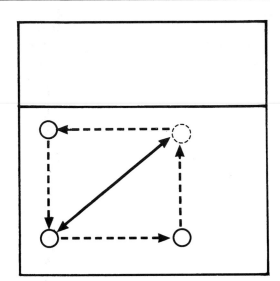

Fig 24

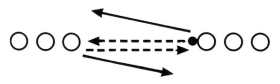

Fig 25

Fig 26

9. In groups of four players; using two balls, two of the players change position after playing the ball. Timing and accuracy are essential (Fig 27).
10. In groups of four with 2m between the two outside players and 4m between the groups; alternate short and long passes (Fig 28).

11. Alternate short passes to the net and long passes across the net. One player has to move under the net to receive the short passes on each side (Fig 29).

COMMON FAULTS

Lifting the Ball

When the ball is played too low in relation to the head, the hands and arms are unable to make the correct shape and play the ball

Fig 27

Fig 28

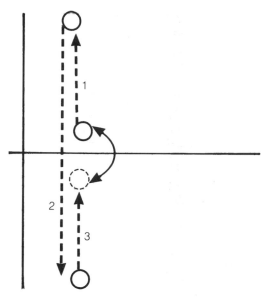

Fig 29

legally. A quick check on the position of the hands is to take the hands away just before contact and see which part of the body the ball contacts. The correct place is on the forehead. If it is lower, the hands were too low and they need to be raised higher or the player move forwards, closer to the ball.

Ball Goes Straight Up

This is another problem caused by playing the ball in the wrong place in relation to the body. This time it is being played directly above the head and the force applied by the hands and legs is directly underneath.

Pass is Low and Flat

If the legs are not used during the pass, the arm action alone may give the ball a flat trajectory. The pass to another player should not go directly at them but at least 5m into the air, so he/she has time to get ready to play it.

THE SET PASS

The setter is volleyball's equivalent of basketball's playmaker – he/she sets up the attack with a volley pass that the attacker hits. This pass is known as the set pass. There are a number of different 'sets' that vary not only in their position along the net, but also in their height above the net.

This variety enables a team to make it more difficult for the opposition to anticipate where the attack is coming from. A lot of responsibility, therefore, rests on the shoulders of the setter. A good setter will read the opposition's strengths and weaknesses, match them with those of his/her team and try to set the ball to give the attackers the best chance of success. The setter always has the right to decide where and what set is made in each situation. The primary aim of the setter is play a good set, one that can easily be hit and that gives the attacker a number of options. If this can be achieved regularly, the setter can then think tactically about the type and placement of the set. Top-level setters also develop the ability to disguise the direction and type of the set long enough to prevent the block or defence from getting into position.

An essential requirement for any setter is good volleying technique, the ability to play the ball legally, accurately and consistently. Peripheral vision is important so that they can quickly work out their position on court in relation to their own and that of the opposition players. Attackers also blame the setter if they are blocked or hit the ball out. An even temperament is essential for a setter.

The Types of Set

The setter and attackers must agree a common system for describing sets. Teams use a variety of different systems based on names, numbers, colours or codes. Fig 30 illustrates the most commonly used numbering system.

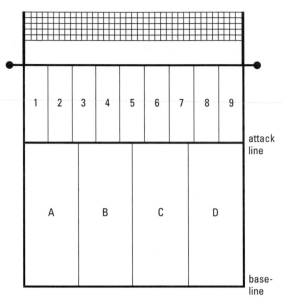

Fig 30 Setting zones.

This divides the frontcourt into nine zones each one metre wide. The setter adopts a frontcourt position around zone 6 about 3m in from the right sideline. The reason for this is that as most smashers are right-handed, as the balls come towards their right shoulder first, they will find them easier to hit.

So the setter can tell an attacker that the ball will be set to a point in the frontcourt – for example, zone 1 on the outside metre of the court on the left side. However, this does not tell the smasher anything about the type of set; its height or speed.

A second level of description needs to be added that refers to the height and speed of the ball. A normal high set 4–6m high to the sidelines is called a 0 (zero). By combining these two codes the set can be accurately described – for example, a high outside set is 10 forward or 90 overhead. In addition to these sets, there are the sets to the backcourt players. The backcourt is split into four zones just over 2m wide, usually called A, B, C or D.

These sets are played to be hit above and just in front of the 3m attack line. Provided the smasher takes off behind this line, they can hit the ball inside the attack zone.

Volleyball is an intensely psychological game. It is a game of chess played at speed with twelve players. Both teams are trying to exploit weaknesses in individuals, line-ups and strategies. Team's attacking strategies include having all three frontcourt players as well as one or two in the backcourt approaching the net to try and keep the opposing defence guessing as long as possible.

Ideally, the setter should have several players making approaches to the net seeking sets in different positions, speeds and heights.

It is also useful to think of the sets in terms of speed. The lower sets are the fastest way to make an attack, the high sets the second and the backcourt the third. At an advanced level, the attack system for a team can incorporate smashers moving to attack all these sets. In these situations coaches refer to first, second and third tempo attacks.

First Tempo Sets

These sets are commonly called the quick or short sets by players. The ball is played close to the setter and only a short distance above the net. The idea is to cut down the time between the setter receiving the ball and the smasher hitting it so the block and backcourt defence have little time to react.

Sets Numbered by Height or Speed
0 = high set 4 – 6m above net height
1 = 30m above net height – short set
2 = 60cm above net
3 = 1m above net

The exact position of the ball in relation to the setter and its height above the net is subject to variation for each individual player. As a rule, the ball is placed an arm's length from the setter; this gives the smasher the chance to angle the approach and increase the area of court that he can attack.

The quickest set is played only 30–60cm above the net to a smasher already in the air with their arm moving down to strike the ball. The setter plays the ball up into the path of the smasher's arm. Alternatively, and this is often used as part of a combination attack by more than one player approaching the net, the ball is set 1.5–2m high close to the setter. You can play either type overhead to the outside smasher in position 2 or for the middle smasher to run around the back of the setter.

When the ball is played low and fast towards the sides of the court, these sets are called shoot sets. Shoot sets are most often played to zones 3 and 4.

Second Tempo Sets

These are played forward to zones 1 and 2 for the smasher in Position 4 and overhead to zone 9 for the Position 2 smasher. All these will be set to a height of at least 4m and land just inside the antennae. The ball should be set about half a metre from the net so the blockers will find it more difficult to contact the ball.

Third Tempo Sets

These are the backcourt sets to zones A, B, C and D. Timing and accuracy is crucial for these to be effective. Ideally these sets are linked in a combination attack where the frontcourt smashers approach for first and second tempo sets and draw the block. This should give the backcourt attacker a clear net to attack over. As the ball will be hit about 2.5m from the net, the smasher has less mar-

---

The Timing of Tempo Attacks

At the time the setter releases the ball:

- the first tempo hitter is in the air;
- the second tempo hitter is taking off;
- the third tempo hitter is starting his approach.

---

gin for error so he needs to have a consistent height and position for the set.

When the setter is under pressure from a poor second pass, they will often use a high ball to the backcourt players as the safety set. On these occasions, the ball will be set higher and often behind the attack line.

In looking at the differences between the various tempos, it is helpful to look at them in terms of the setter's release of the ball. The set release gives the attackers a timing point.

The sequence of photos overleaf (Figs 31–34) illustrate all three tempos used in succession to form a combination attack. The attack is completed by a backcourt player hitting in zone A. Notice that he has taken off from behind the 3m line and legally contacts the ball within the attack zone. Combination plays are an important element of a team's tactical plan. These are considered in this context in Chapter 4.

Tactics

If you are going to be a setter, you need to understand the basic tactical elements of the game and of smashing. Coaches will normally put their strongest attacking players in Positions 4 and 3 as these are best suited to right-handers. The setter, who is often not very strong at smashing as he gets less opportunity to practise, is placed in Position 2 in the front row. This means that the strongest attackers on

Fig 31   The first tempo player takes off for a quick hit as the ball is jump set.

Fig 32   The Play set hitter takes off for the second tempo while the first player is in the air.

Fig 33   The third tempo hitter, a backcourt player, takes off behind the 3m line while the second hitter is in the air.

Fig 34   Having completed the attack, the backcourt hitter lands within the attack zone.

one team are against the weakest attackers on the other. A good setter will try to take advantage of this by setting the ball to Position 4, so that his blockers will be hitting against a weaker blocker. Balancing individual players and positional strengths and weaknesses is vital for a setter. A team revolves around its setter; poor set selection or execution reduces the chances of the smasher winning the rally.

When the first pass to the setter is not very good in terms of its direction, height or speed, he/she should aim to set the ball high and wide as this is the 'percentage set', the one with most chance of success. If, however, he/she has a good first pass, he should take the opportunity to introduce some variety into the attack by setting overhead or playing a short set into the middle. In these situations, the setter must look to see where his players are and if they are ready for this set. Look at the opposition to see if all their blockers are going to be in position – is one of the blockers slow in getting ready, is one of the blockers technically poor or short? With this information, the setter can decide on the type and position of the set. Remember, just because an attacker calls for a particular set, it does not mean he/she must get that ball regardless of whether a more effective set can be made elsewhere.

The team coach and players should establish a system of calls and signs for particular sets or combinations. This way they will all know what is planned, or can be attempted, if the pass to the setter is good. This is the final and possibly the most important thing for a setter to remember – if the first set is good the moves and combinations can be played, if not, the percentage set must be used. There is no point in setting balls that cannot be hit or will inevitably be blocked.

Training

As a setter, you must have absolute mastery of the ball, you must develop such a feel for the

---

Ten Tips to Success as a Setter

1. Talk to your attackers.
2. Keep calm.
3. Get there early and take in the view.
4. Adjust to the situation.
5. Set the situation not the system.
6. Set the individual not the position.
7. Take it high.
8. Turn and face.
9. Set a hittable ball.
10. Follow through into your cover position.

---

ball that you can control its speed and direction almost as accurately as a snooker player controls the balls on the table. You must be able to play the ball on the move, when it is low or to the side. This can only come from hours of practice and self-criticism.

If you want to be a setter, you must have your own ball and practise at home in the garden, in the gym, or anywhere else you can. To develop good ball control you do not need to have a second player, although this can be helpful.

Practices

1. Use a wall with targets marked to volley against.
2. Set up a washing line and put markers on the ground to denote the nine zones. Throw the ball up and set the ball to drop into the zones.
3. Bounce the ball on the ground, move under it and set into a marker, hoop or basketball goal.
4. Throw the ball against the wall, then move under the ball and volley into a marker. Volley the ball to yourself and keep it in the air while you turn round, sit down, lie down, roll over and so on.

SMASHING

For most players the smash, or the spike as it is occasionally called, is the most exciting part of volleyball. All players like to jump up and hit the ball hard into their opponent's court and quite rightly so. The satisfaction gained from seeing the ball go past the block and land in court beyond the reach of the defenders is something that is remembered long after the match is over. However, the smash is very difficult and does not always score. There is a tendency to blast away at the ball without regard to its position or whether there is a block in the way. It is at this point that the difference between a good and an average player is most evident. For the smash is only one of a number of ways of concluding an attack, and choosing and executing the right method is not easy.

In this section, we will look at the smash and its alternatives, the tip, the tactical ball, the offspeed attack. One point that must be emphasized is that in the attack brains are more important than brawn. If you can accept this point you are well on the way to becoming a good attack player.

The smash involves the player jumping to gain as much height as possible and then hitting the ball with the hand across the net and down into the opponents' court. The rules do not allow the player to contact the net during or after the action, nor to throw the ball. On take-off and landing the player may not completely cross the centreline and touch the opponent's court with any part of their body. If you are one of the three backcourt players at the time of the attack, you may not play the ball across the net in any way unless it is below the height of the net or you take-off from behind the attack line before you play the ball. The libero player is not allowed to play a ball at or above net height across the net.

The effect of these restrictions is to force the player to be in control of their body before, during and after the attack. It is a difficult skill to master because it requires a great deal of co-ordination and body control from start to finish.

The smash can be broken down into the following phases: the approach, the take-off, the movements before hitting, and the hitting action and recovery.

Approach

The approach is designed to bring the smasher into the right position in relation to the ball, at the right time. The hardest part for the beginner appears to be getting the timing right, but in fact correct positioning takes longer to achieve.

The correct take-off point is about an arm's length behind the ball with the feet facing in the direction of the intended smash. If this is achieved then every part of the action that follows has a chance of succeeding. Smashing is a cumulative action in that if you get something wrong at the beginning, it is difficult to correct it later.

The starting point and angle of approach varies according to the attacking position, the set that is going to be hit and the attacking system that the team uses.

Normally the angle of approach for a smasher in Position 4 is between 45 and 60 degrees to the net. The middle smasher, Position 3, approaches at a more acute angle of around 60 degrees. A right-hander in Position 2 will approach at a right angle to keep the ball in front of the right shoulder. For a left-hander, these angles will be reversed as their strongest attacking position is on the right at Position 2.

As players and team advance, other attacking systems such as the Swing Hitter system will involve a considerable change in both the starting position and angle of approach. For now, let us look at the technique needed for the basic approach at Position 4 for a high set on the outside, a 10 set.

The approach starts about 4m from the net, outside the court in the area of the junction between the side and attack lines.

Different styles of approach have evolved but all aim to produce a controlled but vigorous two-footed take-off. It is never possible to say that one approach will suit all players but the one recommended here is generally regarded as the most efficient. Normally an approach will consist of four steps or more accurately three steps and 'step close' to finish. This pattern is shown in Fig 35. The higher you can get in the air, the more you increase the potential effectiveness of your smash. This is achieved by generating momentum during the approach and converting it in the final plant and take-off phase into the power needed to gain maximum vertical lift.

Do not forget that the ball determines the start of your approach so you must watch the ball into the setter and during his contact phase. There should be an increase in speed throughout the approach phase.

If you are right-handed, begin the approach with a step forwards onto the right foot (Fig 36). At the end of your approach, you want to end up with the right foot behind the left so that your right shoulder and hip can rotate forward into the ball during the contact phase. If left-handed you will want to achieve the opposite.

The second step with the left foot establishes direction (Fig 37). By now, you should be able to determine the path of the set and the take-off point. This step orientates you towards that position at the same time creating the maximum number of angles and options for the smash. The second step is much longer, probably twice as long as the first and very much faster. Remember you are trying to outwit the opposing block and outpower the backcourt defence. Developing speed in the approach is essential for both. As this step is longer it lowers the body ready for take-off. Keeping a low path throughout the final part

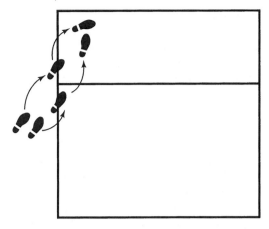

Fig 35   Footwork pattern for smash approach.

Fig 36   The second step is onto the left foot. On the second step the smasher starts to accelerate by pushing hard off the front (left) foot and swiftly bringing the right foot forward.

Fig 37   As the right foot comes forward the arms are forcefully swung back behind the shoulders.

Fig 38   Just after the right foot lands for the third step it is followed by the left foot that is placed just in front.

of the approach enables you to achieve the most efficient leg position in the jump.

On the second step the arms are ahead of your body ready to begin the forceful backswing that helps generate power for the take-off and arm speed in the contact phase. As the weight passes over the left foot move the arms backward with the palms uppermost to achieve an angle of between 45 and 90 degrees with the shoulders.

Drive the right foot forward as fast as possible (Fig 38) into the plant or take-off phase. It should land heel first – facing in the direction of the smash – on this stride to help check forward movement. The final movement is the 'step close' where the left foot moves forward to land facing into the centre of the

court, just in front of the right (Fig 39). Just to remind left-handers, your 'step close' is made by the right foot. At this point, both feet are in contact with the ground and the legs should be flexed so that the strong hip and leg muscles can be forcefully extended to provide the vertical lift for take-off.

Take-Off

Once you have landed with the legs bent, arms stretched behind the shoulders and feet close together, you are ready for the major effort – take-off (Fig 40). The take-off must be fast and vigorous in order to gain maximum power and height for the smash. A good maxim to remember is: 'You can only take out

Fig 39 Both arms are swung upwards as the legs extend.

Fig 40 After take-off, the non-hitting arm (the left one) reaches upwards as the right arm is pulled back.

what you put in.' In other words, a slow, lazy take-off will result in a slow and lazy smash.

Pull the arms down below the waist and upwards as fast as possible. Extend the arms fully above the head before your feet leave the floor. As well as assisting with take-off, the arm pull helps you achieve a balanced position in the air which is essential for control of the hit in the next phase. The arm pull also helps arch the back in the air increasing the potential range of movement in the hitting action.

Preparing to Hit

Draw the arms up above the shoulders and point the non-hitting arm, the left, up towards the ball. This has the effect of assisting the backward rotation of the hitting shoulder and torso, which is useful for creating additional power in the smash. Draw the hitting arm back with the elbow kept high (Fig 41).

The action at this point is similar to the serving action in tennis. There, the arm throwing the ball stays high, as the racket arm is bent at the elbow and brought back. As the left arm rotates down, the right hip rotates forward, the racket arm is extended upwards and forwards to contact the ball at the top of the arc. Substitute the hand for the racket and you have the essentials of the smashing action in volleyball. This rotation of the hips, shoulders and arms ensures that the ball is contacted as high as possible and that the movement of the arms brings the hand down on to the ball, directing it into the court.

41

Fig 41 The hitting arm is brought through with the elbow high.

Fig 42 The ball is contacted with a fully extended arm just in front of the body and hitting shoulder.

Contacting the Ball

For maximum power and control, contact the ball in front of you in line with your hitting shoulder (Fig 42). If you are under the ball, looking up at it as you hit, not only will you lose power you will be forced to topspin it and risk hitting into the block or net.

Make sure you reach as high as possible to contact the ball. Every centimetre counts in volleyball and hitting the ball below your maximum reach is decreasing your chances of success. When the set is less than perfectly placed it is vital that you try to take it as high as possible.

During the armswing phase, pull the wrist back and spread the fingers slightly. As the arm straightens, throw your hand forwards and downwards at the ball. Hit the ball with the open hand, not the closed fist. The hand will mould around the ball if the fingers are relaxed and this will impart a slight topspin to the ball to get it down into the opponents' court. Hit through the ball with the upper body and after contact rotate the elbow slightly outwards, so that the hand and arm will come down without contacting the net.

On landing, flex the legs slightly and immediately look for the ball. Never assume that the smash has been successful as play often goes on and the smasher must be ready to play or block again.

The Smash: Ten Tips to Success

1. **Talk to your setter**
   Let him/her know what set you would like. If he/she or the coach has other plans be prepared to play the intended set.

2. **Watch the pass into the setter**
   This will help you decide whether the set will come to you.

3. **Accelerate to the take-off**
   There can be no half-hearted measures. Once you start your approach, build up speed and momentum as quickly as possible.

4. **Watch your steps**
   Your approach pattern must be timed according to the set that is going to be played to you.

5. **Get a good arm backswing**
   If you want a controlled yet powerful smash you must get your arms well back by the time the feet are planted for take-off.

6. **Lower the body**
   During the approach, lower the body so that at take-off your legs are flexed ready to push upwards.

7. **Pull and push**
   On take-off, pull the arms down from behind the shoulders and take them up above them as the legs push off the ground as vigorously as possible. Remember the power for the smash has to come before you leave the ground.

8. **Point and draw the arms**
   Point the left arm up to the ball as you draw the right arm back. This will facilitate the rotation action that helps hit the ball down into court.

9. **Stretch high**
   Make sure you use every centimetre of height you can achieve by hitting with the arm fully stretched.

10. **Relax the wrist and hand**
    The final part of the action is the wrist snap that gives spin and also direction to the ball.

Practices

The smash is a complex skill when it is taken out of the game situation and a highly complex one within it. The temptation for teachers and coaches is to try to break it down into separate elements and devise non game-related practices to teach it. Volleyball is a game in which the ball is continually moving and the execution of the smash depends on players responding and adapting to changing circumstances. The smash is most successfully taught in game-like practices. This not only speeds up the learning process, but also equips the player better for the demands of the game.

The Arm Action – Practising the Armswing and Take-off

1. Adopt the take-off position with the feet in the plant position, legs flexed, arms extended behind the shoulders. Pull the arms through and jump as high as possible.
2. Start facing – not underneath – a basketball backboard or ring. Repeat 1, but tapping the ring or backboard with the left hand followed by the right.

Positioning the Ball in Relation to the Body

From the start, players must ensure that they hit the ball when it is in front of, not directly above, the hitting shoulder.

3. Stand erect and lift the left arm vertically above the head with the fingers outstretched. Lower it approximately 20cm and move it across the body until it is in front of the hitting shoulder. Raise the outstretched right arm until the two hands touch. This is the normal point of contact for the ball.

4. Mark a point on the floor with chalk, tape or marker. Stand with your hitting shoulder about 30cm behind this point. Hold a ball in your right hand and toss it straight in the air. It should drop on top of this mark. After a few successful attempts keep the right hand in the air after releasing the ball and finger touch it on the way down.

5. Work in pairs at the net. One player stands about 1.5m from the net holding the ball with two hands at waist height, facing the left sideline. The second player stands facing the net. The first player tosses the ball into the air so that it goes about 2m above net height and then drops in front of the right shoulder of his partner.

6. When the toss is accurate, the first player adopts the take-off position, the second player tosses the ball up for him/her to jump to catch the ball two handed as high as possible in front of them. Check that the arms swing properly on take-off and that the ball is caught with outstretched arms at the highest point possible.

7. Repeat 6 but instead of catching the ball draw the right arm back keeping the elbow high. Then hit the ball with the open hand across the net. By starting this distance from the net the player is forced to reach high to get the ball across the net.

The Approach

Remember the approach has two functions. It brings you into position to hit the ball and it helps you maximize the height of your hit. So far, we have learnt how to take-off, position the ball in relation to the body and hit it across the net. Now we need to link in the approach steps.

8. Start a further 2m back from the position in practice 7. Walk through the sequence of steps. Start with the weight on the right foot with the arms back behind the shoulders and step forward onto the left foot. The next part, the 'step close', is the tricky one to grasp. As the weight moves over the left foot, hop forwards off the left foot and complete the step close. The heel of the right foot lands first and as the rock over onto the sole takes place the left foot lands just in front. Complete the movement.

9. Link the full approach with hitting the ball. Initially it is difficult for the smasher to time the approach with a ball set to them and then complete the movement sequence with a hit. It is better for the smasher to make the approach and be fed a tossed ball as they complete the step close. The feeder should stand 1.5m from the net and toss the ball to a height of 4.5–5m. Take-off position should be 0.5m behind the tosser with the right shoulder in line with the dropping ball. This exercise will help the smasher learn not just the full movement sequence but also to time and position the approach.

These exercises introduce the technique of smashing in easy stages. Once you have learnt to smash, the following exercises provide training for accuracy and control.

10. The basic training exercise for smashing is the feed into the setter in position 3 or the

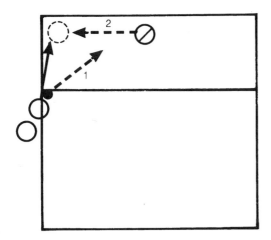

Fig 43

When the game is fast and the setter has to make quick decisions, they need to know that you will arrive at the right time and in the right place. Being in the right place is more than just the relationship with the setter, it means having a body position and attitude that will enable you to see the blockers, the court and the options open to you.

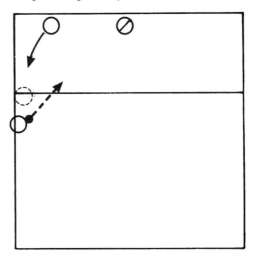

Fig 44

standard setting position between positions 2 and 3, followed by a set to the waiting smasher (Fig 43).

11. As before, but get a player in the centre of the backcourt to feed the ball into the setter. This helps to learn the timing of the approach.
12. After hitting the ball as in the previous exercise get the player next in line to feed a second ball to the setter after the first ball has been hit. Start at the net and get the ball fed into the setter by the next player in the line. The smasher jumps up to block and then returns to the 3m line to start the approach (Fig 44).
13. A ball is smashed softly from position 2 and the smasher digs the ball straight to the setter before smashing (Fig 45).

Hitting the Quick Attacks

Although the fundamental technique for hitting the quick attack is the same as for other types of set, the timing and positioning requirements are different. As the middle hitter you will have many changes of position during a set or rally but you must develop a consistent approach and timing with your setter.

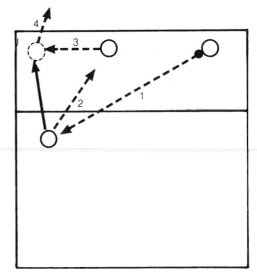

Fig 45

45

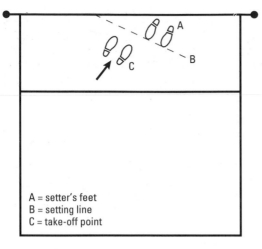

A = setter's feet
B = setting line
C = take-off point

Fig 46 The quick hitter should take-off 60–100cm from a line drawn between the net and the setter's feet. The ball itself is contacted on this line. This position enables the setter to put the ball up above his shoulder and the attacker to have room to turn on the ball if necessary.

During the rally you must keep adjusting your position in relation to the setter and the ball so you can move in quick when a smash is on. Whereas the setter will normally try to set from a position at right angles to the net, for the quick attack they will open out a little to get a better view of your approach.

When you contact the ball you should be almost parallel with the setter. Fig 46 shows the relationship diagrammatically. Your approach may have less steps than when hitting on the outside as you will be working in a more confined space and you want to make the attack process as quick as possible. Also for speed you will find that a shorter armswing and drawback prior to hitting are helpful. Get your hitting arm up early so that the setter can have a target to aim at.

With good co-ordination the setter will be playing the ball directly up into your hand as you bring it through to the contact point. The best position in relation to the setter for you will be at an angle of approximately 45 degrees to the net. Most of your shots will go on the diagonal but if you drift to the right of the ball you can use shoulder or wrist rotation to direct the ball into the middle or cut it back towards Position 1 in backcourt.

Contact is with a very shortened action at the highest point, basically a wrist snap onto the ball. Speed, control and direction, not power, are the priorities for a successful hit.

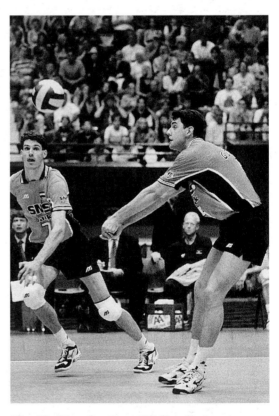

Fig 47 Van der Goor (Holland) times his approach for the quick hit with the pass by Gortzen. Notice how Gortzen has angled himself towards the setting zone and is focused on guiding the ball to the frontcourt setter.

Fig 48   Olikhver (Russia) attacks the ball set by Usakakov (11). Notice how the hips have rotated forward leading the shoulder that will come through with the arm to give power to the shot. The two blockers are focusing now on the contact point trying to move to cut off the path of the ball across the net.

Fig 49   Russell 11 (England) drives the quick hit down into the Scottish block. Notice the finish point of the arms that come down close to the body to avoid the net.

Fig 50   Bitencourt of Brazil executes a classical tip over the three-man Russian block.
Notice also the concentration of the outside two blockers on the smasher and ball. The third
blocker has moved his arms across to cut off the low inside angle.

Alternatives to the Smash

The Tip (Fig 50)

The tip, or dump as it is sometimes called, is a very useful shot to perfect. Use the tip to catch the opposition unawares; just when they are expecting the ball to be hit hard into the back-court, play it softly into the frontcourt area.

The element of surprise is important, so all the actions before contacting the ball should be similar to those of the smash. At the last moment, stop the arm and play the ball on the fingertips.

The Offspeed Attack

When the faster sets in the centre and outside positions are used it is not always possible or necessary to hit the ball hard. If the ball is hit on the side with a cutting action it will travel sharply down into court. The defenders will be expecting a hard smash and often will not be able to move fast enough to stop the ball hitting the floor.

49

CHAPTER 3

Defensive Skills

In this chapter you will learn about the techniques for making the first touch of the ball after your opponent plays the ball into your court.

One of the strange things about volleyball is that to be successful you need to be stronger in defence than attack. When a team wins a rally, it serves the ball to its opponents, who then have all the advantages. They know where they are going to make the attack, what type of attack it will be and which of their players will carry it out. Analysis of the game has shown that the side making an attack has a seventy per cent chance of success in the rally. In order to win a point, the serving side has to beat the odds first in the rally as their opponents make the first attack.

All players naturally prefer to concentrate on developing their attacking skills as these are the skills that bring the crowd to their feet; but there is, I believe, as much pleasure to be had from defending a smash successfully. After all, you can only smash balls that get to the front of the court. If your team's defence cannot give good passes to the front you cannot smash anyway. The defensive skills are: the dig pass, backcourt recovery shots and the block.

In recent years, the beach game has had a substantial influence on the indoor game. With only two players on the beach court, the players have a greater area to defend. Consequently, they tend to defend much further in court to cut out a larger proportion of the backcourt. The smashed ball will be taken earlier and therefore higher than it can be effectively played with the forearm dig pass. To do this, the ball is played overhead rebounding the ball off the fingers and hands.

A relaxation of the handling rules on the first play of the ball by the receiving teams in the indoor game has allowed this overhead technique to be used not only to receive the smash, but also to receive the serve. Although some teams and players aim to receive the majority of balls overhead, many feel that the accuracy levels are less than the standard forearm pass. Both coaches and players need to make their own choice based on an assessment of the quality of pass achieved in the game situation. What is clear is that all players will need at some time in the game to use the forearm pass so they must develop good technique. Certainly at beginner level, I would advocate teaching and playing using the forearm pass. It is a vital technique that will be needed in a variety of situations.

THE FOREARM PASS

The forearm pass, sometimes called the bump pass in North America, is used in two game situations. Firstly, it is used to receive the serve and play the ball to the setter in the frontcourt. Secondly, it is the main technique used to play the opponents' smash and in this situation is often called the 'dig pass'. As the serve and smash are played at different speeds and angles there is a variation in the technique needed to play the two shots.

Receiving the Serve

The pass from receive of service to the setter in the frontcourt is normally called the 'first pass' and is of fundamental importance to the team in that rally. A good pass is one that controls the speed of the ball, plays it to the correct area on court for the setter and has a trajectory that will make it easy for him/her to give a variety of sets. If the pass is poor in any aspect, the quality of the attack that the side can make will be affected.

The Keys to Successful Passing

These are:

1. getting into the right court position to play the ball;
2. at the right time;
3. with the right body posture.

Apart from the jump serve, the ball is rarely travelling at a great speed and it is usually easy for you to anticipate the direction of the serve from the court position of the server, the angle of their body and your experience of earlier serves.

The tactical formations chosen by teams aim to place the best receivers in positions where they can easily move to play the ball (*see* Chapter 4). Some formations employ specialist receivers and move the other players out of the passing area. However, even if you are not the chosen specialist you need to acquire a good level of passing skill as you will still have to play some serves and smashes.

Reception of service starts the moment a rally ends. It is vital that you forget the last rally and focus on the next. Get into your court position well before the server gets back to the serving line. Look at the server to try and pick up clues from their position on court, the distance they are from the baseline and their stance to gauge the type of serve they will use and the intended direction. The earlier you can successfully predict the trajectory of the ball the more time you have to get into the best position to play it.

Stance (Fig 52)

The team's reception formation should put you into a good starting position for the ball. You will then need to ensure that your stance not only allows you to move to the point of impact but also gives you a good body position to execute an accurate pass. When moving to the ball use small shuffle steps rather

Fig 52 The basic stance for the dig pass. The player must be ready to move quickly in any direction to play a variety of techniques.

51

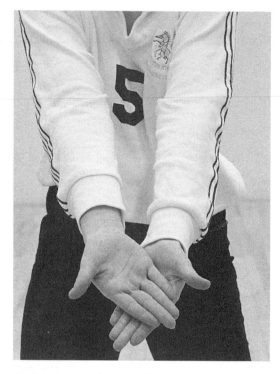

than long or crossover steps. This keeps you balanced and gives you the opportunity to fine-tune your positioning, especially when playing a floating serve.

One foot is kept slightly in front of the other because most of the movements to play the ball will be either forwards or backwards. Legs should be flexed, with the head and shoulders up. If you have to move towards the ball, try to keep your body at the same height as you move instead of moving up and down. Your arms act as a guide to the positioning of the body in relation to the ball, so they must be kept straight and in front of the body. Resist the temptation to stand with your hands clasped together. Keep them apart at waist level just outside shoulder width. You will be able to move your arms into the path of the ball followed by the rest of the body.

Hand Grip (Figs 53 & 54)

A firm platform to play the ball is vital to a good pass. As soon as possible before the moment of impact, lock the arms at the elbows to make a straight line from the wrists to the shoulders. Play the ball on the fleshy insides of the forearms. Grip the hands together to make sure that both forearms are parallel, providing a wider platform for the ball. It must hit both simultaneously if a good pass is to result. Place the fingers of the right hand across the fingers of the left hand then bring the thumbs together so that they are touching along the outside edges. When the ball is played, push the hands down to open up a long smooth surface on the forearms for the ball.

ABOVE LEFT: *Fig 53 To play the dig pass, the hands are placed across each other with the arms locked at the elbow.*

LEFT: *Fig 54 The thumbs are brought side by side, giving a firm rebound surface for the ball.*

Do not try to play the ball by interlocking fingers, as this is not only slower to form but also puts the hands in the way of the ball. Try making the correct grip quickly by putting the thumbs and forefingers of each hand together and then sliding the hands inside each other. It is most important that forming the grip becomes automatic and not something to think about just before the ball is played. This is the part, that, if played incorrectly, becomes painful. The arms are acting as a rebound surface for the ball and not a striking implement. If the arms are swung into the ball as though they were a bat, not only will the pass be poor but also the arms will hurt.

When the ball is served hard, it will often rebound off the arms sufficiently to reach the setter. Otherwise, you can give it extra speed by pushing upwards and forwards with the legs as the ball is played.

Playing the Ball (Figs 55–57)

Accuracy of direction, height and speed of the pass are vital to allow the setter the maximum setting options.

Always aim to play the ball in the mid-line of the body. If your arms move outside this line the ball may not contact both forearms and fly off at an angle. Most players find it a little easier to play the ball slightly to the right of the actual mid-line but still within the base provided by the feet. Should it be necessary because the ball floats on service or you misjudge the point of impact, to play the ball outside the body, lower the shoulder nearest the

ABOVE RIGHT: *Fig 55 The legs are flexed, one in front of the other, with the straight arms in the 'mid-line' of the body.*

RIGHT: *Fig 56 The hands are kept at waist height and well away from the body. As the ball is played, the weight is transferred from the back foot and the legs extend upwards and forwards.*

Fig 57 Contact is made just above the wrists on the forearms.

setter so that your arm platform is angled behind the ball.

The angle of the arms to the shoulders for a ball played in the middle of the court is normally approximately 45 degrees. This angle gives a good arc to the pass to the setter. As you get nearer to the net then the arms will move nearer the horizontal to increase the lift and decrease the forward movement.

Remember the serve is moving towards you and if you are still moving towards it at the point of impact the result will not be a smooth controlled play of the ball but a collision! It is essential that you get into a stationary position

---

Ten Keys to Successful Passing

1. **Focus on the server**
   As soon as the rally ends, focus on the server, his/her court and body position.

2. **Be ready early**
   Adopt the ready position, arms in front, legs flexed, shoulder-width apart, eyes on the server.

3. **Move with shuffle steps**
   Focus on the served ball as you move, using short, shuffle steps that help you keep a strong balanced position at all times.

4. **Keep arms out in front**
   Stretch the arms in front of the body at waist height and use them to line you up with the serve.

5. **Stop before you play the ball**
   Try to make a firm plant of the feet with the arms in position before you play the ball. This gives you a strong platform on which to play the ball.

6. **Keep the ball in the mid-line of the body**
   Play the ball in the centre of the body for more control and accuracy. If you have to play it to one side, drop the inside shoulder to angle the arms behind the ball.

7. **Rigid platform**
   Keep the arms straight from the wrists through the elbows to the shoulders.

8. **Get the angle**
   Before you contact the ball, line your feet and shoulders with the target point so that you will not have to swing at the ball.

9. **Feel the ball**
   Each serve has a different angle and speed. You must try and develop a feel for the ball so you can add or take away speed as necessary.

10. **Steer it**
    Control the ball – don't let it control you. Steer it with your legs, hips, shoulders and arms to the setter.

with the ball lined up with the centre of your body, the arm position already formed, and the shoulders angled towards the setting target before the ball crosses the net.

On contact, you can take the power out of a hard-hit serve by pulling the arms back very slightly towards the body. This has the effect of cushioning the serve and 'kicking' it up into the air with a little backspin. For other serves move with the ball in the direction of the target point. Try to steer the ball with your whole body not just an arm swing. This way you will begin to get the necessary feel for the ball and have control of it.

The setter wants to be able to play the ball about one metre from the net between front-court positions 2 and 3. In top level play, they want a fast pass in at net height so they can jump set for a faster attack. At other levels of play, you should give them a little more time to assess their setting options by passing the ball in a loop at least 4m high.

The Dig Pass Receiving the Smash

The smash is hit much harder than the serve and also, as it is hit close to the net, much steeper. The technique for receiving the smash must be adapted to these conditions. Another factor that must not be ignored is that once the ball has been struck, it will have landed before a defender has time to move. The defender must have already decided the direction he expects the smash to take and worked out, from the distance of the ball from the net and the height at which it will be hit, whether it will land short or deep in court. Although this sounds almost impossible, an experienced player will gradually recognize the signs that will help him to make these predictions. If the ball is set back off the net then it will land in the backcourt and vice versa. The higher the point of contact with the ball, the steeper the ball is likely to be hit.

Stance
The defensive formation your team plays will limit the area you are expected to defend. As the ball is hit so hard you will have no time to move forward to play the ball once it has been struck. All you can hope to do is to cover the area to the side and in front of you that you can reach by stretching.

One of the consequences of adopting the more relaxed rules of the beach game in relation to playing the ball direct from the serve or smash has been that the defender is allowed almost total freedom in keeping the ball off the floor. As long as he does not catch and hold the ball the first official will probably let play continue.

As with passing the serve, some players aim to play the smash on the hands above the head while others use the forearm pass. Those in favour of the overhead pass tend to defend nearer the net so that they can narrow the angle in the same way that a tennis player approaches the net. This does mean that there is very little chance to play anything other than the overhead pass. There is no doubt that there are situations when the overhead pass is more than adequate or is the only way of playing a smash when it comes from an unexpected direction or situation. But as with passing the serve there is a greater accuracy and flexibility with the forearm pass.

Place your legs just outside shoulder width with your knees turned in slightly. Keep on the inside of your feet, because this will make it easier for you to move sideways to the left by pushing off the right foot and vice versa. Keep your weight forward with your hips just ahead of your heels. A helpful tip is to make a slight backward movement with both feet, approximately 10cm, as the smasher takes off. This will bring your weight forward and make movements to the ball much quicker and easier. If the ball falls in front of you, it is also easier to fall forward

Fig 58 Gortzen of Holland is in an ideal position to play the ball. Arm platform well formed, low body position, weight forward, hips and feet angled into court towards the setting zone and superb concentration on the ball.

onto your knees and stretch your arms under the ball.

You must start from a low position. Not only will this give you more time to play the ball, it will enable you to get your arms under the ball and bring it up into a good pass to the setter.

As you may have to quickly move your arms to either side, they must be kept up and clear of the knees. Prior to playing the ball, put them together and form a platform for the ball. If the smash is very hard, you may have to take some of the power out of the ball by withdrawing your arms slightly on contact.

Just as you did with the receive of service, angle your hips and shoulders towards the setter's frontcourt position before you contact the ball.

Keep your head up and watch! There is so much for you to look at, the movement of the ball and players around the court, your frontcourt blockers, the set, the smasher's approach, position and timing. With the information you obtain you should be adjusting your court and body position. More information about the tactical aspects of individual backcourt defence can be found in Chapter 5.

This part of the game is often called floor defence which is a good description. It is your responsibility to commit yourself to preventing the ball from hitting the floor.

To play the backcourt successfully you must not be afraid of going onto your knees or the floor. A well-padded pair of kneepads is absolutely essential. Injuries in volleyball are extremely rare but playing without kneepads can result in bruising or abrasions that are unnecessary.

BACKCOURT RECOVERY SHOTS

Most smashed balls will be played in the backcourt below knee height. Many times the ball will either rebound off the block or another player, or your opponents will place the ball out of reach. In these situations it is often not possible to use the dig pass, and more spectacular techniques are called for.

There are three main recovery shots that must be acquired: the forward dive, the roll and the sprawl. Each has its use in different game situations. One of the great things in volleyball is to see players diving and recovering balls that seem certain to hit the ground. Once again we owe a debt to the Japanese, who pioneered these techniques and so successfully exploited their amazing agility and

determination in backcourt. Every national and club team has copied them and this is now an important part of the modern game.

Although these techniques look spectacular they are not dangerous. Volleyball is an exceptionally safe yet spectacular game.

The Forward Dive

This is the best technique to use when the ball is dropping well in front or even to the side. It involves diving forward, reaching out with the hands and playing the ball upwards on the back of one hand. Immediately after playing the ball, the hands reach down to the floor and take the body weight, as the player lands first on the chest and then the stomach.

Tips for the Dive

1. Move forward as far as possible then push off and dive forward and slightly upward.
2. Stretch your arms forward and try to get a hand under the ball. When the ball is to the left use the left hand and vice versa. For safety reasons do not cross hands.
3. Just before contact drop your hand and then raise it quickly to hit the ball into the air on the back of it.
4. Lower both hands to the ground keeping your chin up so that it will not contact the floor.
5. Arch your back with your toes high; this will stop the knees and feet landing uncomfortably.
6. Lower your body slowly onto the floor so that your chest followed by stomach and thighs touch the floor. If you have kept your toes high the knees will hardly touch the floor.
7. Allow yourself to slide on the floor so that less strain will be put on the hands.

Fig 59   *Having kept the ball in the air by using the back of her hand the Chinese player cushions her landing with her arms and thighs.*

The Roll

This is mainly, though not exclusively, used by female players as they sometimes find that the dive needs too much strength. There are, however, many occasions when this is the most suitable way to play the ball whether you are male or female.

It is normally used for playing balls to the side, but when, for example, the ball has been tipped over the block near the sideline, the ball can be played back into court by using this action, after running forward and turning slightly (Fig 60).

The Roll

1. Stretch as far as you can towards the ball so you are as close as possible to the floor.
2. This will straighten the inside leg.
3. Starting with your arm behind the shoulder, swing under the ball and towards the target.
4. Play the ball on the heel of the hand or the closed fist swinging the arm up and towards the target.
5. This will bring your shoulder onto the ground. Allow the rotation to continue and roll over into a crouched position ready to continue with the game

Fig 60 Lima of Brazil covers behind the block. By rolling outwards he will not only keep the ball off the floor but direct it back into court.

The Sprawl

This technique is used to increase the defensive area that a player can cover. With this technique, the area covered by a defender is that which can be reached by sprawling flat on the court with the arms extended. The idea is to place the arm or back of the hand under the smashed ball whether it is to the side or in front of the player. The ball will then rebound back into play.

It is essential to start with the basic defensive stance, the same as that for digging the smash. If the ball is going to land in front, drop down on the knees and stretch the arms out to contact the ball. This may involve going onto the chest as well. If the ball is to the side, push off the opposite leg and stretch towards the ball.

Practices

Receive of Service

1. Dig ball continuously in the air, aiming to keep ball under control.
2. Dig ball continuously against wall, to hit the wall at least 3m off the ground
3. Bounce ball on floor and dig rebound.
4. In pairs; one player volleying, one digging.
5. In pairs, one player under basketball or netball ring, volley ball to partner 3m away, who tries to dig ball into ring.
6. Player A throws ball over to B who digs to C. Ball is passed back under net. As players get more proficient, speed up their exercises by using two balls (Fig 61).

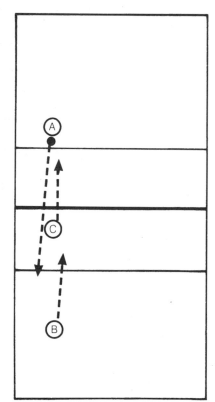

Fig 61 Drill.

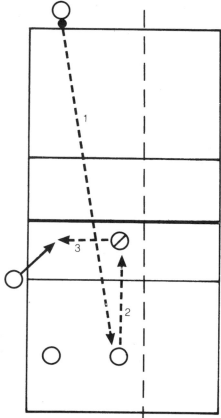

Fig 62 Drill.

7. Split the court into four sections with a server, two receivers, setter and attacker in each court. Serve the ball, dig to setter, smasher runs in, jumps up and catches the ball and rolls it back to the server on his baseline. Each group works independently (Fig 62).

Receive of Smash

1. In pairs; one player receiving ball, the other feeding the ball by softly playing the ball from as high as possible down to knee level of his partner. Gradually build up until the ball is fed with a soft smash.
2. Three feeders and player; player comes on court from Position 5, digs a soft smash, side-steps to the next position and repeats (Fig 63).

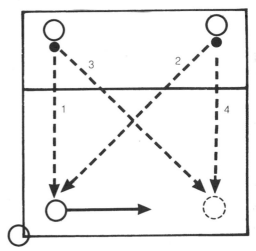

Fig 64 Drill.

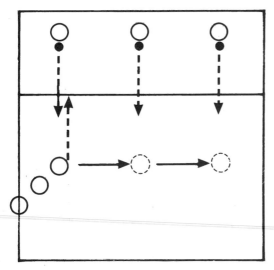

Fig 63 Drill.

3. Each player receives four balls smashed softly at him in the order shown. The ball is played back each time to the smasher; after playing the first two balls, sidestep across to Position 1 (Fig 64).

4. With two frontcourt smashers, the player in position 5 digs the first smash across court to Position 2. The smasher then moves across to Position 1, receives a ball, smashed diagonally from Position 4 and digs it to Position 2. These movements replicate the game situation where the setter waiting to receive the pass is in Position 2.
5. In threes; this is a pass and follow smash, dig and set drill. The first player volleys the ball to a player 3m away and then follows the pass. The second player smashes the ball and also follows his pass. The third player digs the ball and the drill continues. Control, quick court movement and early preparation are essential in this drill (Fig 65).
6. One player smashes at three backcourt players in Positions 1, 6 and 5. The player waiting immediately replaces the player who digs the ball. Again an exercise in control, movement and preparation (Fig 66).
7. The same starting line-up as exercise 6, but the three backcourt players continue the exercise for a three-minute period. After playing the ball, the player changes places

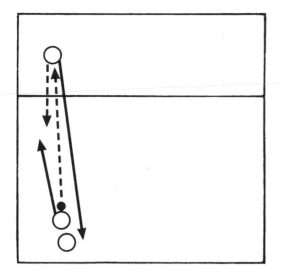

Fig 65   Drill.

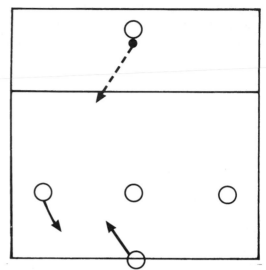

Fig 66   Drill.

with his neighbour before the next ball is smashed. If the central player receives the ball all players keep their places (Fig 67).

This technique can only be mastered by starting from the correct defensive position with the weight forwards, otherwise it would be impossible to move quickly enough to play the ball.

THE BLOCK

The power of the smashers in the modern game is so strong that unopposed they make it very difficult for the backcourt defenders to play the ball successfully. To try and stop the smash crossing the net, the opposing front-line players jump up and place their hands in the path of the ball to block it. When the ball is blocked directly back into the smasher's court ending the rally – commonly known as 'stuffing' the ball – it gives a psychological boost to the team. When the smasher makes the next attack he will split

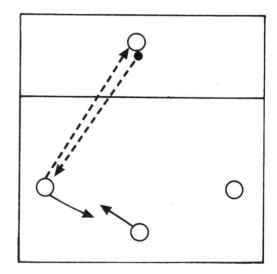

Fig 67   Drill.

his concentration between hitting the strongest shot he can and making sure he passes the block.

At the highest level, teams must have a strong block to have any chance of success. Good blocking is more than stopping some of the attacks completely and winning the rally. It is also taking the pace off balls that are not stuffed, and channelling shots that pass the block into the defensive cover.

When the attack is made at the side of the court, teams will use two blockers – the outside player and the centre player. For attacks through the middle they try to use all three players but this is not achieved very often as the centre attack is made very quickly.

You may only block the ball if you are a frontcourt player and only contact it after your opponents have completed their attack. The net may not be touched during the block and you have to be very careful that, in your keenness to get the ball, you do not brush the net on the way up, as you reach across or on the way down.

Successful blocking relies on good positioning, good timing and good technique – luck rarely plays a part. Just as with other volleyball skills, preparation is the key to success. The blocking action starts as soon as the ball passes into the opponent's court and not when the smasher starts his approach.

You must look at the position of the ball and try to identify the attacking options open to the setter. Look for the frontcourt players and try to predict the shot they are expecting to be played. Teamwork at this stage is vital; you must let your fellow blockers know what you see happening. Particularly when teams are using combination attacks, it is only when the blockers have the bigger picture that they can decide which position, which set and which player to block.

THE BLOCKING LINE-UP

Where you stand to block depends upon your playing position in the frontcourt. Each player has individual blocking responsibilities that vary according to the opposition attack strategy, individual attackers or the blocking strategy adopted by his/her team.

Left-Side Blocker – Position 4

As the opposing attacker in this position is usually the setter, there are fewer attacks from this side. Unless the smasher in this position is left-handed, most attacks will be played towards the centre of court or diagonally to Position 1. The left-side blocker should start one metre in from the sideline to cut out these shots and offer the attacker the difficult line shot. This blocker also has to cover attacks made by the middle attacker behind the setter and warn the other players when number 2 moves around for a cross-over attack in the centre.

When the opposing team have a frontcourt setter in Position 2, the left side blocker can move into the centre to help the middle blocker take out the quick hitter. He/she must still be on the look-out to stop the setter playing the ball over on the second touch.

Middle Blocker – Position 3

The middle blocker should position himself/herself opposite the setter to be in position to block the quick hitter. He/she has to have good communication with the two outside blockers so that he can move out to help them and vice versa.

Right-Side Blocker – Position 2

This player has responsibility for blocking the opposition's main power hitter in Position 4. They should start a metre in from the sideline to cut out the diagonal. At the same time they must be ready to move to the middle to block the opposition's number 2 crossing over behind the quick hitter in a combination attack.

Fig 68   Van de Goor of Holland is in an ideal ready position to block the set.

THE BLOCKING ACTION

The blocking action itself can be broken down into the following phases: finding the line, timing the jump, playing the ball, and the recovery.

Finding the Line

Once it is clear where the set is going, look at the angle of the approach of the smasher and not the ball. The smasher is aiming to hit the ball and will be in the right place. By watching the smasher, you will have more chance of blocking the ball.

Smashers hit most shots the way they are facing; this gives greater accuracy and power. Watch the approach line of the smasher to determine whether he/she intends to play the ball across court or down the line. The outside blocker is responsible for 'setting the line' and the middle blocker moves to block alongside.

If the block is placed directly opposite the ball it is still possible for the smasher to hit past it. The outside blocker should try to position their outside shoulder directly in line with the hitting shoulder of the smasher. If the smasher tries to hit the ball on the diagonal not only will they have to pass both hands of the blocker, the centre blocker will be in the path as well.

While waiting for the smasher you should be at the net with the legs flexed, shoulder-width apart and the hands just above head height outside the shoulders (Fig 68). The middle blocker's hands should be higher to cover the quick attack. Stand about 30 cm from the net ready to move to either the left or right into the path of the smasher.

To maximize the area you can cover with your hands above the net, rotate your wrists outwards and spread the fingers so that the largest area possible is in the path of the ball. The hands should be slightly apart to increase the blocking area, but make sure that the ball cannot get through.

Moving to the Blocking Position

The speed and variety of the attack requires blockers to respond quickly and move into position quickly. Particularly when a blocker is moving to form a two- or three-man block the footwork should enable the blocker to move and stop in a balanced and controlled manner.

When the distance that the blocker has to move is up to 2m, the simple side step (Fig 69a) is quick and effective. If, however, the middle blocker has just blocked on the right side and the opposition have set up the ball for an attack on the left, the cross-over step (Fig 69b) or pivot step (Fig 69c) pattern may be quicker.

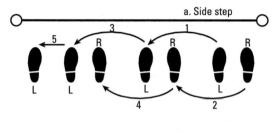

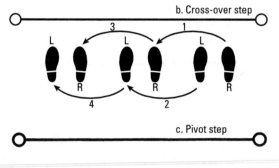

Fig 69   Blocking step patterns.

At the end of the movements you should be balanced and able to take off on both feet.

Timing the Jump

If the blockers jump at the same time as the smasher, they will find that the ball passes over them as they start to go down. This is because it takes some time for the ball to cross the net after being hit. When blocking the ball on the outside, with a ball set within 1m of the net, take off after the smasher. However, when the ball is set off the net it will take longer after being hit to reach your blocking position so you must delay your take off. If the set is within 1–1.5m of the net, take off as the smasher's arms swing upwards on his/her take-off. If the ball is set even further off the net, wait until the smasher is in the air and just starting to swing his/her arm forwards to make the hit. Obviously these guidelines need to be adjusted to suit the jumping heights and speed of individual smashers and blockers.

The middle blocker should be waiting with his/her hands almost vertical opposite the setter. As a short set is made, he/she should take off so that his/her hands are right over the ball as it is hit. If the arms penetrate over the net, the smasher will have very little chance to direct the ball around the hands.

To get maximum height on the jump, dip first and then vigorously extend the legs and arms upwards. When you dip, try to keep your arms extended, this will mean that as soon as you get off the ground they are above net height, therefore increasing the potential blocking time.

Some players like to pivot away from the net so they can use an arm swing to gain extra height and then turn into a square position on the net. If they are the outside blocker they can do this without interfering with the second blocker. However, this technique cuts down the time the arms are in the blocking zone above and across the net. It is up to coaches and players to judge the effectiveness of this style in individual cases.

Playing the Ball

Earlier it was emphasized that you need to read the game and assess the most likely place the attack will be made as the build-up begins. Once you are in the air you need to make lots of decisions if you are going to block that ball. The first priority must be to keep your eyes open (Fig 70)! It is surprising how many players, as soon as they take off and reach net height, shut their eyes as they reach for where they think the ball will be.

Your arms can reach across to penetrate the opponent's court space. By moving your hands towards the ball you reduce the passing angle. However, just penetrating is not enough: you must have your hands at the same height as the

Fig 70 Keep your eyes open when you block. Van de Goor is concentrating on the attacker's arm so can adjust his arm position as necessary.

Blocking: Ten Keys to Success

1. **Early preparation**
   As soon as the ball is in the opponent's court, start assessing the setter's options.

2. **Identify the location of the smasher opposite you**
   Their movements are the key to your blocking position on court.

3. **Communicate with your fellow blockers**
   Call out the shirt numbers of the frontcourt players, tell them if you see a player moving into position for a combination play.

4. **Look at the smasher first, then the ball**
   Once the set is on the way the smasher will concentrate on getting into position to hit it. You should line up with the smasher's approach before looking at the progress of the set.

5. **Keep your arms up and body balanced**
   You need your arms in the blocking zone as soon as you leave the ground to maximize your potential blocking time. Always take off vertically from two feet.

6. **Adjust your timing to the set**
   If the ball is near the net, take off as the smasher begins his/her jump; if it is further away, jump as he/she starts the arm action. The timing for each ball is individual.

7. **Keep the outside hand facing into court**
   Make sure the smasher cannot play off your hands out of court by turning the hand inwards, and on contact pressing towards the centre of the court.

8. **Penetrate the net**
   Don't just block high, get your hands over the net. This cuts down the passing angle and ensures that the blocked ball stays in their court.

9. **If you can't stuff it, play it up**
   If for any reason you are unable to get over the top of the smash to play it down, relax the hands and try to take the pace off the ball by playing it upwards into your backcourt.

10. **Where is the ball?**
    If you have not contacted the ball you must look for it as soon as you can. It may be landing quite near to you or have been deflected towards you from the backcourt.

ball will be at that point. If your opponent contacts the ball high above the net you will have to reach up which will have the effect of reducing the distance you can penetrate. Conversely, if they hit it low, you can get closer.

Remember that you cannot contact the ball until the smasher has made contact and to be careful that, in your desire to penetrate the court you do not touch the top of the net.

Even though you may have your hands directly in the path of the ball, success is not assured. The smasher may attempt to play off your hands and out of court so make sure that the outside hand is angled into court. If you are caught out of position and do not directly front the attacker, it is not a good idea to move your arms across outside the line of your body to try and cut the ball off. They will not be penetrating the net so the ball could be played down on your own side losing the point or the ball will be deflected causing problems for the defence. In this situation you should block vertically which will at least cut off that part of the net should the ball be played there and the defence will have a clear view of the shot and a chance to get into position.

Fig 71   Blange and van de Goor (Holland) force the smash down for the point. The hands have penetrated the net, the blockers have locked their arms, tensed their stomachs and piked as they contact the ball to drive it down.

In your starting position the arms are just outside shoulder width. As you go to block, bring them in towards the ball. This action helps to close around the ball and direct it inwards and downwards. Just prior to contact, shrug the shoulders to increase the range of your arms and tighten the stomach muscles to keep the body firm. Now is the time to look for the ball and to try and 'cap' the ball with the hands. When the ball contacts the hands, the wrists are pushed down to force the ball down into court (Fig 71).

There are times, such as when blocking a backcourt smash or a particularly powerful high-hitting smasher, when the blocker should take the pace out of the ball rather than try and block it down. To do this the hands are kept high and the fingers relaxed. The ball will then rebound upwards into the blocker's court giving the backcourt time to play the ball.

Recovery

After contact with the ball or when sure the ball has passed, pull the hands and arms backwards to clear the net. Once they are back across the net, bring them down to shoulder level ready to block again. The legs should be flexed on landing and you should immediately turn to look into court for the ball. Although you may not have contacted the ball, a player behind or even the other blocker may have made contact and it might be falling just within reach (Figs 72 and 73).

Blocking is the only occasion in the game when a player may have two consecutive touches. The block is also unique in that it does not count as one of the three touches each team is allowed. After the block has touched the ball, a team may still play it three times in the normal way. If the block touches the ball and it lands

Fig 72   The Italian blockers have not stopped the Japanese tip.

Fig 73 As soon as they realize the ball has passed the block, they turn to look for it. Fortunately Busetti the 'libero' player has reacted quickly and retrieved the ball.

out of court, this touch is then counted and the opposing side wins the rally.

Blockers should try to learn which are the smashers' favourite shots, what timing they use, when and where they like to tip the ball – everything that can be learnt about a smasher will help to improve the blocking. Backcourt players can help by telling the block if their line or timing was incorrect. Volleyball is a team game and blockers must seek and accept the advice of their team mates.

Practices

1. Two players face each other on either side of the net. Take it in turns to walk from the 3m line to the net at a 45 degree angle. One player stays at the net and moves into the path of the incoming player's hitting arm as in blocking.
2. The player walking in jumps and throws the ball gently across the net and his partner attempts a block.
3. In pairs; one player holds the ball up close to the net for partner to jump and block. If necessary, the player with the ball can stand on the bench.
4. As exercise 3, but the player throws the ball up close to the net for the partner to block.
5. In pairs; one player throws the ball up close to the net to his left and right for partner to move to and block (Fig 74).

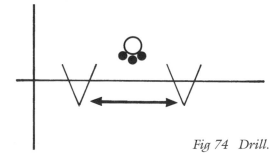

Fig 74 Drill.

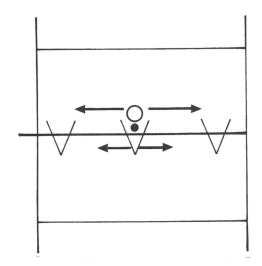

Fig 75 Drill.

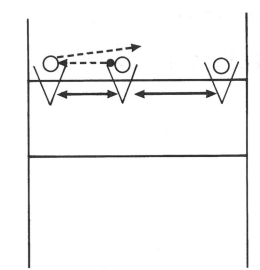

Fig 76 Drill.

6. Three blockers at the net and one player with the ball. The player with the ball moves along the net and blockers cover him. When the player stops, he/she jumps up and plays the ball into the hands of the blockers. A two- or three-player block is formed depending on the position of the ball (Fig 75).
7. There are three players on each side. One group volleys the ball between themselves and blockers form up opposite the player with the ball. To give the blockers time, the ball must be passed quite high (Fig 76).
8. Two players block against a smasher. The centre blocker can only move to the outside when the set has been made.

Common Faults

Touching the Net
On take-off, this may be because the arms are swinging upwards instead of extending vertically or blockers are trying to reach over too early. Check that after the blocking action the arms are pulled back enough to clear the net on the way down.

Ball Rebounds out of Court
If it goes to the side, the hands are not facing inwards and the smasher is taking the opportunity to play off the block. If the ball goes over the end line, the jump was a little too late so that the hands were not over the ball at the time of contact.

Ball Passes round the Block
Either the wrong line has been set or the smasher has skilfully used the wrist and hand to turn the ball around the side of the block. The backcourt defenders will be able to tell the block if the correct line was chosen.

Ball Drops between Blockers and Net
The hands must reach over the net so that on contact the ball will drop on the other side of the net.

CHAPTER 4
Team Play

Strategies

In this Chapter you will learn about the strategies that teams use to create strong attacks and defences in the game.

Although there are six players on court for a team, they must not be considered as six individuals but as a united six, drawn from the twelve players each team is allowed in its squad. Every player in volleyball is totally dependent on his/her team-mates who play the ball before and after him/her. If you make a mistake in volleyball you cannot, as in football or basketball, chase after the ball and try to retrieve it or make amends. You have one instantaneous contact that must be right, first time. It is important that volleyballers understand and accept this fundamental facet of the game. They must learn to accept the mistakes of others and be prepared to admit their own without qualms. If players cannot work together, then the team will not function as a co-ordinated unit, and its performance will be adversely affected.

Volleyball is a very psychological game – teams try to put players under pressure and force them to make mistakes. When they do, they will continue to force that player to play the ball in the hope that this will lead to either a substitution or a breakdown of the opposition's game.

In-top class games, in particular, you will see players encouraging their team-mates when they make mistakes as well as when they win a rally. The player who has made the mistake will often raise his/her hand to acknowledge that he/she was responsible for losing the rally. Players on the bench are quite prepared to come onto court for just a few points to bring a new dimension to the tactics or to give another player a break. The whole squad participates in a match, not just the players on court.

Volleyball is not an easy game to coach, because the coach has to try to use the strengths of his players to their full advantage in circumstances that are continually changing as players rotate positions with service. Tactics can be as complex as those in chess, with less time in which to make decisions. Coaching a team is like conducting an orchestra. If the instruments or players are not working in harmony, the result can be most unsatisfactory. To obtain success in volleyball, players must not only have good technical skills, but the willingness to work as part of a team.

Choosing a Team Strategy

A team strategy must co-ordinate receiving of service, attack and block defence formations. Formations must be chosen that will integrate, so that player movements are kept to a minimum. There is little time for positional changes during rallies. The formations must be related to the skill level of the team, as well as the individual players involved.

For receiving the service and the attack phases there are literally hundreds of alternatives but the ones detailed in this chapter are suitable for teams both starting out and those with limited experience. It is nice for players and teams to say that they play advanced formations and use complicated movements, but the ultimate criterion is whether the percentage of successful plays is increased by playing the more advanced systems or not. If the percentage is lowered then no matter how spectacular the formations look they are not suited for your standard of play.

Roles of Players

Although William G. Morgan had the notion that volleyball should be a game without specialists where the rotation system gave everyone a chance to play all aspects of the game, the modern volleyballer has become a specialist.

Therefore, team formations are driven by the need to get specialist players into their optimum positions. The names given to the specialist players vary according to the tactical strategy. Fig 77 lists current names and their role in the game.

Although players have to start the rally in their normal rotational positions, the frontcourt setter will try to move to Position 2 as soon as the ball is served. Middle and outside hitters also move to their specialist positions.

Service reception line-ups are designed to facilitate these moves. The players on the serving team can move as soon as the ball is served.

Overlapping

The rules of the game include the 'overlapping' rule that is designed to keep players in their front and backcourt rotation positions (Figs 78 & 79). When the game was invented, very few tactical formations were used and this rule was simple to operate. Coaches have now devised formations that stretch the rule to the limits and it is essential that players have a full understanding of the rule. At the time the ball is served, the players are considered to operate a system of pairs in relation to both their neighbours in the rotation and the players opposite them in back or frontcourt.

Role	Game Position
Setter (S)	Plays in Position 2 frontcourt and Position 1 backcourt
Outside or Release Hitter (RH)	Plays in Position 4, hitting balls in the front left side of the court
Quick Hitter (QH)	Plays in Position 3 and acts as a middle blocker
Play Set Hitter (PH)	Plays in Position 2 and moves to other central positions in combination plays. In the starting line-up is opposite setter
Libero (L)	Plays only in the three backcourt positions but cannot serve
Swing Hitter	In the swing hitter system he/she receives the serve and starts his/her attack from the centre of the court
Universal (U)	Plays opposite the setter as a hitter or second setter if needed

Fig 77 Players' specializations.

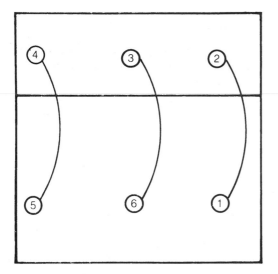

Fig 78 Overlapping vertically. The back player must be behind his/her opposite number in the frontcourt at the time the ball is served.

BELOW LEFT: *Fig 79   Overlapping horizontally.*

BELOW RIGHT: *Fig 80   This unusual service receive line-up is legal and gives the team several options for a combination attack involving all three frontcourt players.*

The player in rotation Position 5 must be behind Player 4 and at the same time to the left of Player 6. Player 6 must be behind Player 3 and to the left and right respectively of Player 1 and Player 5. Within these

---

Overlapping – Tips

- Once the ball has been served, any player can move to any position on court.
- Do not waste points by being penalized for overlapping. Make sure both feet are behind or to one side of your 'pair'.

---

restrictions, the players can adopt any position on court. Fig 80 illustrates an advanced formation that is legal. By studying it closely, it can be seen how the rule has been stretched to the limit.

The only occasion when the overlapping rule does not apply is when a team is serving. As the server can serve from any position along the base-line, they can legally overlap with another backcourt player at the time of service.

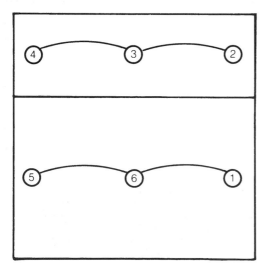

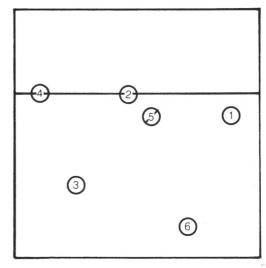

Whether two players are overlapping or not is determined by the second official, the official working at court level. This official will check that there is a gap between the line of the players' feet. The exact positioning is very complex and coaches should tell their players to make sure that both their feet are behind or to the side of the other player so they will not lose points unnecessarily

Penetration

When the frontcourt setter is used there are only two attacking points on the frontcourt, which makes it easier for the opposition to prepare their defence. If the frontcourt setter is to be used as a third attacker, a player in the back court must act as the setter by 'penetrating to the front and setting the ball. After setting the ball, the penetrating setter returns to the backcourt ready to defend. Teams using this system must not only have very good setters and smashers who can utilize the opportunity to attack from all three positions, but when they receive service they must be very good at digging.

Most infringements of the overlapping rule occur when the back-row setter moves forward before the ball is served.

OFFENSIVE SYSTEMS

The type of offensive system is determined by the number of hitters and setters and is numbered accordingly.

4–2 System

Four players will be hitters and two players act as setters. The setters take their places diagonally opposite each other in the starting line-up (Fig 81). This means that there is always one setter and two hitters in the front row.

5–1 System

One player acts as setter throughout the game with the other five players acting as hitters. When the setter's rotational position is in the backcourt he/she can penetrate and set to three frontcourt hitters. The frontcourt player in Position 2 must be prepared to set the ball in an emergency.

6–2 System

There are two specialist setters who penetrate when they are in the backcourt and act as the third hitter in the frontcourt.

Offensive systems run off the receive of service or as a counter-attack after the opponents' attack has been received.

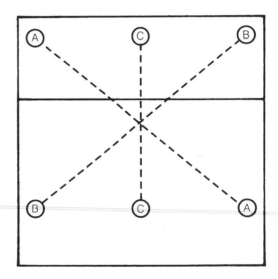

Fig 81 The two setters in a team are placed opposite each other in the starting line-up, so that one is always in the front court and one in the back, and there are always two other players in rotational positions between them.

SERVICE RECEIVE FORMATIONS

The object of a service receive formation is to get the best possible first pass to the setter so that the team is able to have a good chance of winning the rally. Remember every rally lost after receiving the service is a point to the opponents. Mistakes are therefore very costly and the formation chosen must reduce these to a minimum.

At this point, it is necessary to consider how the six players on court are placed in relation to each other at the start of the set or game. Most club teams will play the 4–2 system with two setters and four smashers. At more advanced levels, some will play the 5–1 or even 6–2 systems.

The basic receive formation for the 4–2 system is the W + 1 (Fig 82). Five players are involved in receiving the service and one, the setter, is in the frontcourt to receive the first pass and set up the attack. When the front-court setter is in Position 2 or Position 4, a slight alteration to the basic formation is needed (Figs 83 & 84).

Referring back to Figs 83 and 84, as soon as the server strikes the ball, the setter can run into his setting position. The five receivers all cover a part of the court. The three front players cover

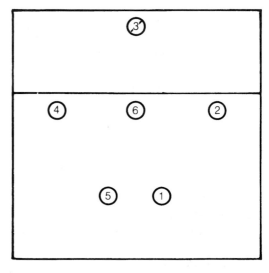

Fig 82 Basic 'W + 1' service receive line-up.

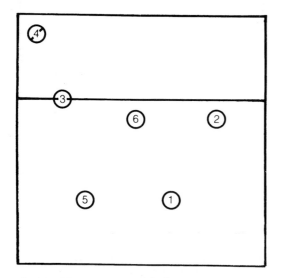

Fig 83 W + 1 system with the setter at Position 4.

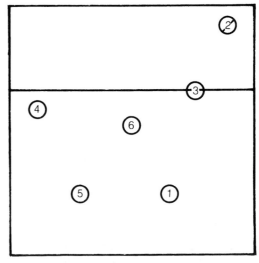

Fig 84 Setter at Position 2 in W + 1 system.

all the short serves and balls they can play by taking one pace back. The two back players then cover half of the remaining area each. It is essential that in this and all other receive formations the player who is intending to play the ball calls 'mine', to avoid two people going for the same ball or players expecting someone else to take it. When the ball is going out of court, it is helpful if the adjacent player shouts 'out', as it is sometimes difficult to judge this when preparing to play the ball.

The receive formations shown so far have all assumed that the setter will set from the middle position. For new teams, this is easiest as the setter has less distance to play the ball and receivers will find it easier to direct the ball into the centre of the frontcourt.

The next stage, and this should only be attempted when the setter is skilled enough to set the ball the full width of the court and the receivers are more accurate with their passes, is to set from Position 2½. Teams can now use the centre of the court as an attacking position.

Setting from 2½ will involve some adjustments to the basic W+1 line-up and this is shown for all three frontcourt rotations in Figs 85–87. Again, the overlapping rules must be observed.

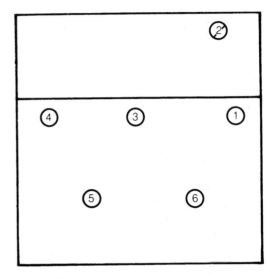

Fig 85   Setter at Position 2½.

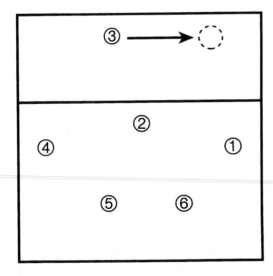

Fig 86   Setter at Position 3 moves to 2½ as ball is served. Attacking player at Position 2 moves forward to play a shot in front of the setter.

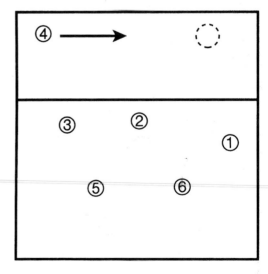

Fig 87   W +1 line-up, with setter at Position 4 switching to Position 2½ to set.

The most difficult formation occurs when the setter is in rotation Position 4 as there is a much greater distance to cover 2½. It is often helpful to get the receivers to dig the ball nearer the centre of the court and, if necessary, first set from Position 3 and then move right across into Position 2 ready for the next rally.

5–1 and 6–2 Systems

Fig 88 shows the receive line-up when the backcourt setter in Position 1 is used. As soon as the ball is served, the setter moves forward into Position 2½ to set the ball forwards to 4, 3, or overhead to 2.

The receivers will cover the same parts of the court as they did with the W + 1 formation, but Player 6 must remember to move to the left after playing the ball to allow the setter to return to the backcourt defence.

When the setter is starting at Position 6, the formation shown in Fig 89 can be used. If the team is using two specialist setters, they will very often not use a penetrating backcourt setter in Position 5. Fig 90 shows a

line-up for penetrating from Position 5 and it can be seen that the setter will have a long way to go to Position 2½ and will also run across the view of several receivers. Top-class setters

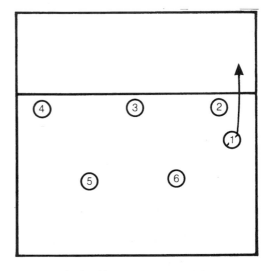

Fig 88   The backline setter at Position 1 penetrates to set the front from Position 2½ as the ball is served.

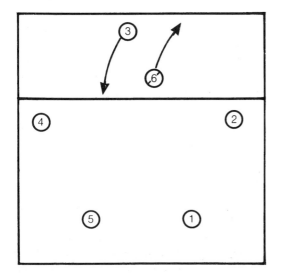

Fig 89   Penetrating setter in Position 6.

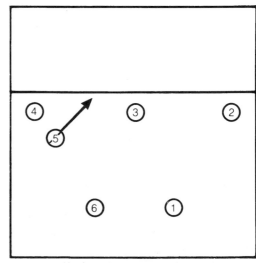

Fig 90   Penetrating setter in Position 5.

and a good receiving team can play this line-up, but most teams combine penetration from Positions 1 and 6 with the standard frontcourt setter at Position 2.

Once the team using penetration has played the ball into the opposition's court, the setter retreats to Position 1 in backcourt no matter whether he/she started from there or Positions 5 or 6. From Position 1, he/she can penetrate during subsequent rallies (Fig 91). Coaches and teams should at all times question whether they are achieving 'side outs', that is, regaining the serve quicker using penetration than using frontcourt setters. The method that gives the highest percentage of successful receives of service rallies is the one that should be employed.

In Chapter 3, the Attacking Skills, the quick sets and combination attacks were discussed. At receive of service the opposition's blockers are already watching, ready for the attack. This is the main time when teams will employ these sets and attacks. Starting from a receive formation means that it is easier to organize the attackers but as the block and backcourt defence are set up waiting for the attack the need for some deception is very important. Teams should aim to get into position to receive service as quickly as possible, and the setter and attacker should communicate by voice or preferably signal the move they want to play.

Two-man Receive

As the game becomes faster and teams want to develop a more varied attack, they need a reliable and accurate pass into the setter and the ability to allow their smashers to attack at different tempos in different court positions. In the process of moving to their final attack position, they will disappear behind other players and then reappear, making things difficult for the block.

Specialist passers can take the majority of serves and develop the extra reliability and

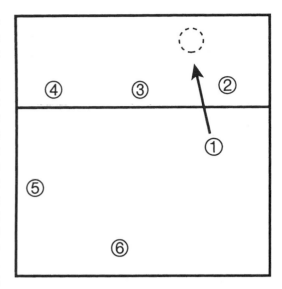

Fig 91   Penetrating setter during a rally.

accuracy that is needed. Teams can play with two or three specialists but most have two main specialists and a third who will help in certain situations. The two specialists are positioned diagonally opposite each other in the rotation and normally play as the outside hitters. Teams can adjust the line-up to suit their players or offensive plan but Figs 92–97 show one series of line-ups. It is important that you study how these line-ups avoid breaking the overlapping rule. Throughout the series the same two players will receive the serve although their court positions will change as they rotate. Possible lines of attack are shown but these are not the only opportunities or combinations potentially available.

Combination Attacks

If a team makes its attacks with just a straightforward high set to the outside and a quick attack in the middle, the opposition blockers and defence will have little to think about. They can be in position early and the smasher will face a strong block and a well-positioned defence.

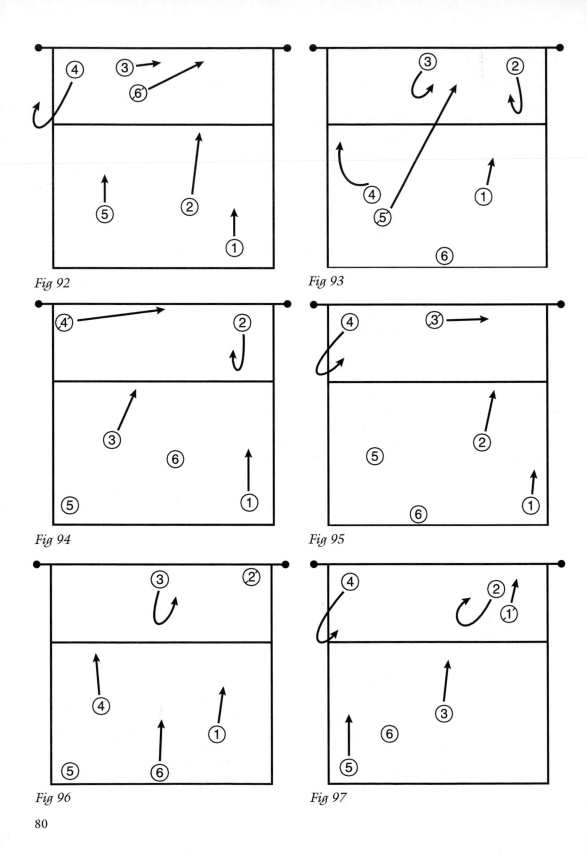

Fig 92

Fig 93

Fig 94

Fig 95

Fig 96

Fig 97

One of the great features introduced into the game by the Japanese in the 1960s was linking several players together in an attack, where the final attack position and type of set was unclear until the last moment. Blockers are then held in a position expecting an attack and cannot move across to another position in time. Alternatively, they go up against an attack that is not completed, leaving the net area free for the actual attacker to play over.

The combination attack is now an integral part of the game at most levels using players in Positions 2 and 3 with possibly a backcourt hitter as well. Position 4 is used for the 'safe' ball when the first pass has been poor or where a one-on-one situation has been created.

To make these sets work the smasher has to get into the right place at the right time by adjusting the angle and speed of his approach. The setter has to be aware of the players around him/her, their timing and approach angles as well as the position of the ball. It is the setter who has control, who can decide which set is the right one to be played in a particular situation. Inevitably, many combinations have been developed and played by teams. Which ones a team uses depends on many factors, not least the ability of smashers to play and time them.

Essentially, we are looking at an Outside Hitter (OH) on the left side in position 4, a Quick Hitter (QH) in the centre and a Play Set Hitter (PS) on the right side or centre. Figs 98–101 show some combination options. Sets are described by numbers (*see* pages 33–4).

OPPOSITE PAGE:
Fig 92 Two-man line up, setter at Position 6. Positions 5 and 2 act as receivers.

Fig 93 Two-man line-up, setter at Position 5.

Fig 94 Two-man line-up, setter at Position 4. Positions 3 and 6 act as receivers.

Fig 95 Two-man line-up, setter at Position 3. Positions 2 and 5 act as receivers.

Fig 96 Two-man line-up, setter at Position 2. Positions 4 and 1 act as receivers.

Fig 97 Two-man line-up, setter at Position 1. Positions 3 and 6 act as receivers.

Arrows indicate possible movements to attack.

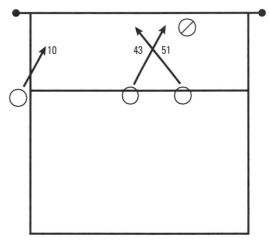

Fig 98 Cross-over attack Sets 10, 51, 43.

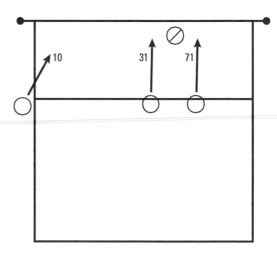

Fig 99 Double Quick Sets 10, 31, 71.

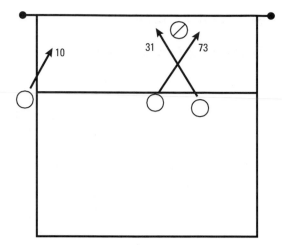

Fig 100   Reverse cross Sets 10, 73, 31.

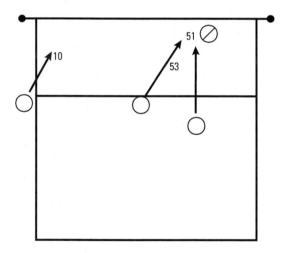

Fig 101   Tandem Sets 10, 51, 53.

Combination attacks depend partly on deception; so receive line-ups can help by locating players in positions where they have a number of alternative routes to the net.

The swing hitter system developed by the USA men's teams in the 1980s was a radical approach to the game. Two specialist passers are used with the frontcourt passer becoming the Swing Hitter. With this system, the attack builds up from the centre of the court and swings outwards compared with the standard attack where the outside hitters begin outside the court and move in. This system forces the outside blockers into the centre to cover the quick and combination attacks and they have to move outwards to block the outside hits. Played at its most complex level, this is a system way beyond the capabilities of most club teams but coaches can adapt it to the skill level of their team.

DEFENSIVE FORMATIONS

Although a volleyball court is relatively small and there are six players on court, it is still difficult to defend. Certain formations have been developed that will give the best court coverage against the attack. All defensive formations have some weaknesses and the coach has to match the formation to both his team's defensive ability and the opponents' style of play. At the top level, teams will adapt their defensive formation rotation by rotation according to the individual smasher and the style of attack.

There are two stages of defence in volleyball; at the net and in the backcourt. In Chapter 3, we looked at blocking as an individual defensive skill but a team can deploy its blockers in a number of different ways.

Net Defence

The standard blocking system has each of the blockers taking responsibility for the attack zone in front of them. Their primary function is to stay in that position until they are sure that the attack is coming from elsewhere. Then they should move to either support the adjacent blocker, or move back off the net into their backcourt defensive position. This system ensures that smashers are confronted by at least one blocker and is good against teams who do not use combination plays. When a team has a frontcourt setter and only two hitters, the blocker in Position 4 should start in the centre next to the middle blocker to cover the quick attack.

When opponents are using combination attacks, the blocking system needs to be able to cover the increased options. This can be done by adjusting positions, 'committing' blockers to particular options or 'reading and reacting' to the game.

If a team is running plays including shoot (31) and overhead sets (71 or 72), the blockers can be pulled in closer together. The blocker at 4 stands in position fronting the reverse 71 set, the middle blocker the quick hitter and the blocker at 2 fronts the shoot 31 set. If the opponents run these attacks they have at least one blocker against them and probably two; if they play the outside sets 10 or 90 the blockers will still be able to get to them.

Commit System

When a team has a strong line-up that is consistently able to run a quick attack, the middle blocker concentrates entirely on the incoming player and commits himself to going up to block. The other two blockers are left to join in the block in the centre or take out their opposite number on their own.

Read and React

In this system, all blockers try to block all attacks. Instead of concentrating on the opposition attackers, they concentrate on the pass into the setter, the setter's movements and the set trying to 'read' the game; to put themselves in the position of the opposition's attackers. They then 'react' and move to the blocking position and time their block according to the set (Fig 102).

BACKCOURT DEFENCE

The Starting Defensive Position

The block is the first line of defence and the second, the backcourt, is built around it. There is the assumption that the block will close off an area of the backcourt. If the block involves two or three players then the area covered increases and the defence needs to adjust accordingly.

Once the ball is in the opponent's court, the defenders should move to their starting or base defensive position. All defensive formations are fluid and take their final shape according to the attack that is made, and the positioning of the block. It is important for the team and players that the base position is achieved as early as possible (Fig 103).

The two wing defenders in Positions 1 and 5 should position themselves almost parallel with the sidelines facing into court. By adopting this position rather than one parallel with the baseline, passes, particularly from hard-hit smashes, will be directed into court rather than out of court. They are also in a better position to make sideways movements to get into line with the cross-court attacker or to chase down a ball played off another defender. By starting about 2m from the attack line, they are in a good position to defend the quick attack, or the ball played over on the second touch.

The central defender's position is shown in Fig 103 as deep but in the '6-up' system, they would be centrally placed behind the attack line and the wing players would drop back towards the corners (Fig 104). The defensive formations differ mainly in how they cover the area immediately behind the block. Some formations have a player permanently behind the block (2–1–3) and others (2–0–4) rely on individual defenders to cover 'channels' which include behind the block.

Fig 102   Meoni and Gravina (Italy) 'reading' the jump set by Blange (Holland) before 'reacting' and choosing a blocking position.

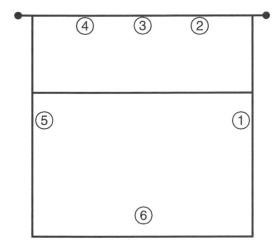

Fig 103   Starting defensive positions.

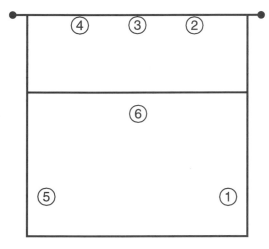

Fig 104   Starting defensive positions with Position 6 up.

2–1–3 SYSTEM

At beginner and lower club levels, a lot of balls will be played just over the block because the poor first passes and sets mean that it is impossible to make a good smash. It is sensible to adopt a system that covers this area well. The most commonly used system is known as '6-up' (Figs 105–108).

The central defender (Player 6) moves up to the attack line and covers the area behind a block in any position, playing balls tipped over or around the block.

When there is a two-man block at the side, the free blocker moves back to the attack line to cover balls angled inside the block either smashed or tipped as well as balls falling that way off the block.

The opposite backcourt player moves to a position where they can see on the inside of the centre blocker, the ball and attacker. The strongest smashes are usually played along this line.

The backcourt player behind the block moves to a position to the side of the block so that he can cover balls hit straight past the block.

When there is an attack through the centre, the two outside blockers should attempt to join the block; if they cannot, they should move back off the net to the attack line and help defend. The two outside defenders should position themselves to the outside of the block. No. 6 will have to decide either to stay in position if the block is well formed, or move back into mid-court to defend if it is not.

The highest level teams who have a tall strong block providing a good block shadow also use this system, with slight amendments. With the powerful smashes in the men's international game, defenders are often unable to control the ball accurately. The backcourt setter playing defence in Position 6 is well placed to play the second touch.

The weaknesses of this system at beginner level are soon apparent. Firstly, the block will often be badly formed and many smashes will get through to the centre of the backcourt and score. Secondly, Player 6 will often be tempted to intercept balls that are better played in the backcourt.

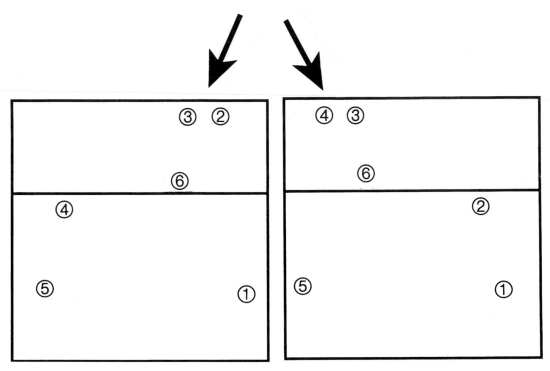

Fig 105   '6-up' cover for attack on the right.

Fig 106   '6-up' cover for attack on the left.

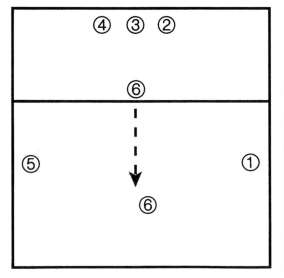

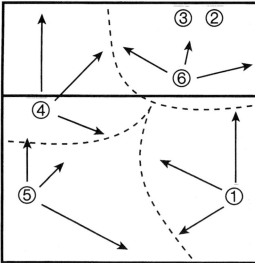

Fig 107   '6-up' cover for attack in the middle
No. 6 position depends on formation of block.

Fig 108   Defensive responsibilities in the
2–1–3 system.

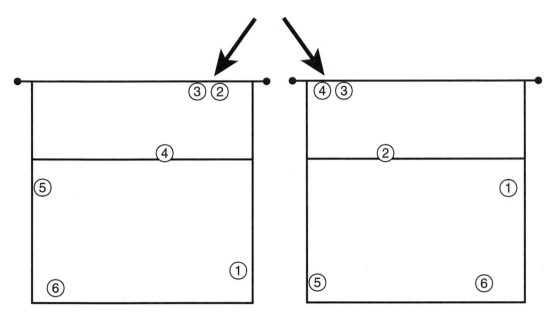

Fig 109   Wing or slide cover for attack on right.

Fig 110   Wing or slide cover for attack on left.

Wing or Slide Cover

In this system the middle back player No. 6 stays deep in backcourt. Responsibility for covering the tip rests with the non-blocking frontcourt player (Figs 109–112). The backcourt

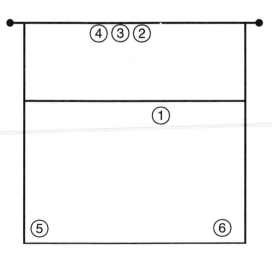

Fig 111   Wing or slide cover for middle attack.

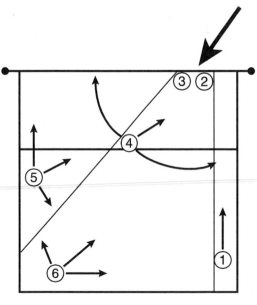

Fig 112   Wing or slide cover – defensive responsibilities.

player behind the block Position 1 or Position 5 will stay back covering deep line smashes. Responsibility for covering the cross-court shot is the middle back player in Position 6. This means that for the attack on the right No. 5 must push up the left side line to cover the power smash on the inside of the block and No. 1 does the same for left side attacks. When the attack takes place in the middle, the frontcourt setter drops back to cover the tip.

This system works well against a team that tips many balls, but if the free blocker does play the ball, it can compromise the attack options for his/her team as he/she is out of his/her normal attacking position.

Man-Up or Rotation System

This system concentrates on defending against a team that hits a high proportion of balls deep into the corners. When the attack is on the right the backcourt player behind the block moves up to cover the tip and the rest of the defence rotates to fit in behind (Figs 113–116). Position 6 rotates to cover line shots to the corner. Depending on which side the attack is made, the wing back opposite the attack takes the cross-court shots and the free blocker swings back behind the attack line to play smashes inside the line of the block.

This system gives you strong tip coverage but the remaining two backcourt players and the non-blocker must rotate into position to give full court coverage. Unlike the Wing or Slide defence, if the free blocker plays the ball it should not impair the development of the full range of counter-attack options.

2–0–4 Perimeter Defence System

The 2–0–4 system has two blockers, no players behind the block and four defenders. If

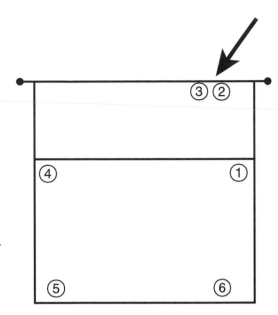

Fig 113 Man-up or rotation system attack from right.

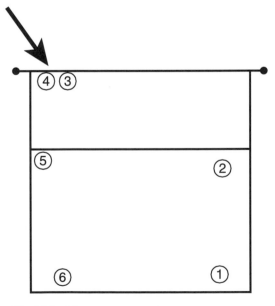

Fig 114 Man-up or rotation system attack from left.

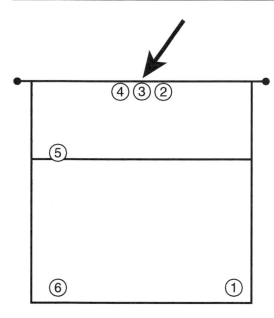

Fig 115 Man-up or rotation system attack from centre.

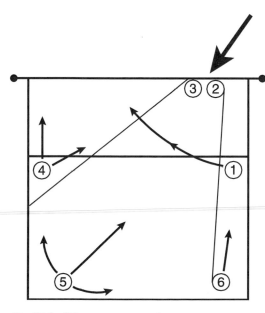

Fig 116 Man-up or rotation system responsibilities.

defenders are experienced and fast-moving and have good recovery techniques, then this system can be used successfully. It is designed to counter deep smashes that form the highest percentage of shots at good club level and above (Figs 117–120).

In this system the centre back player stays deep on the base line and has responsibility for playing balls that are played back off the block, or hit deep to the corners. Their movement is mainly lateral. In effect, they are a 'sweeper'. If a centre attack is made and the block is not closed, they must also move forward to cover the smash in front of them.

When the attack is from the right, the left back Position 5 covers the hard-hit power shot on the inside of the block. He must line up so that he can see the inside shoulder of the blocker, the ball and the attacker's hitting arm. Offspeed attacks played along this line and towards the centre are also his responsibility.

The right back Position 1 is responsible for balls hit down the line, the tips and offspeed balls behind the block and towards the centre. Balls played deep to the corner are the central defender's responsibility.

The non-blocker (No. 4) takes the hard-hit angled smash, tips inside the block and balls coming off the block or net in his area.

In this system, players must watch the attacker, anticipate the shots open to him and move into the best defensive position to cover these before the ball is hit.

To be successful, this system requires all players to be alert, to understand their defensive responsibilities and to communicate with each other. There will be times for example when No. 6 and the line defender could both play a ball. A system of calling for the ball is essential, as is the ability to adjust the system during a match to cover the attacks of a particular smasher.

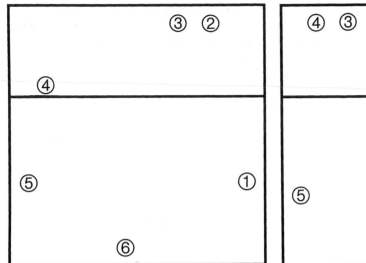

Fig 117 2–0–4 Perimeter defence
against line attack on right.

Fig 118 2–0–4 Perimeter defence
against diagonal attack from left.

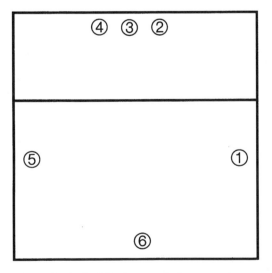

Fig 119 2–0–4 Perimeter defence against an
attack through the middle. Player 6 will go
forward when the block is well formed, and
stay back when the blockers are not together.

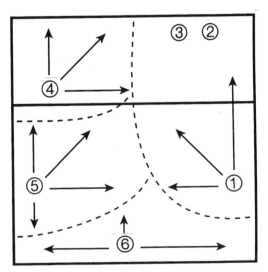

Fig 120 2–0–4 Perimeter defence
responsibilities.

Covering the Smash

It cannot be assumed that the smash will pass the block; in many cases, there is very little chance if the block is ready and waiting. Teams must expect the ball to be blocked back into their court and try not to let the ball hit the floor. Defending in this situation becomes progressively more difficult as the attack increases in complexity. Systems alone will not deal with this situation; it requires a commitment to preventing the ball touching the floor.

A general cover system that will suit teams of most standards is shown in Figs 121–122. This aims to get two rings of cover, one in the immediate vicinity for balls blocked steeply and a deeper one for balls rebounding up off the block.

The player behind the wing smasher and the inside player have the main responsibility for balls that fall close to the net. If these two players start in a low position near the attack line, then any ball that they can be expected to play will be in front of them. In particular, the inside attackers must come back away from the net in order to keep the ball in front of them. The middle back remains in the deep defensive position and the remaining two players cover balls blocked diagonally.

When there is a combination attack, it is not always possible for all players to cover the actual attack. The important point is that cover of the smash is seen as an essential part of the work of the team and that whenever possible the attempt is made to cover. It can be very galling for the blockers just as they are about to celebrate their success, to see a defender keep the ball in play.

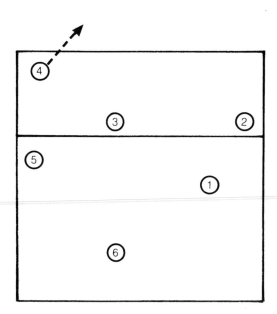

Fig 121 Cover of the smash on the left.

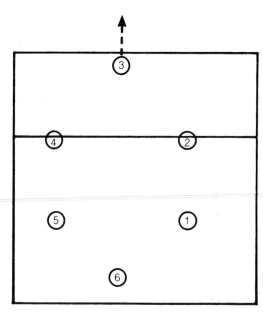

Fig 122 Cover of the smash in the centre.

Fig 123 Great Britain receive on two players 2 and 8 (Positions 4 and 1). The setter No 1 penetrates from Position 5.

BUILDING A TEAM SYSTEM

Coaches have to build a system that will cover all the aspects we have dealt with so far: receiving service, making the attack and defending the opponents' attack (Figs 123–125). Elements of different formations can be linked together, particularly in receiving service, but the coach must consider the movement patterns of his players as they transfer from one part of the game to another. A team system that involves players taking a long time to get ready for each phase is a poor one. One of the difficult yet appealing things about coaching volleyball is that it is not possible to take a complete system 'off

OPPOSITE TOP: *Fig 124 The Latvian middle blocker uses a pivot step to move to the outside position.*

OPPOSITE BOTTOM: *Fig 125 Jones (15) attacks at Position 2 against the Latvian 2–0–4 perimeter defence. The blockers have their eyes open and the centre blocker moves to cut off the diagonal. Britain forms a 1–2–3 cover defence of the smash.*

the peg'. Each team and its players are at a different stage of development in each phase of the game, and the coach must experiment, analyse the results and build a system that suits his team.

Training Practices

If a coach wishes to introduce a new system or modify an existing one then he must make sure, by use of a blackboard as well as placing players on court, that everyone fully understands the theoretical basis of the system. Once this has been done, the players must practise it under a controlled situation. There are many ways this can be done depending on what has to be learnt.

1. Put six players in the correct tactical situation and feed a slow lobbed ball over the net for them to play through as in a rally. Gradually speed up the movements and increase the difficulty of the feed. Ultimately the feed should be from a realistic game situation, for example service or smash from the opposition.

2. Have two teams on court both practising the same tactical situation but from the opposing viewpoints, for example, the serving side preparing to block and defend and the receivers making the attack. Do not rotate the teams or change over servers until it is clear that all the players understand and are trying to carry out the tactics correctly.

3. Use the situation outlined in Exercise 2, but score each rally on a plus and minus system. When a side wins the rally, it gains a plus and if it loses, a minus. Depending on which element you wish to emphasize, make the team playing that part of the game the team that scores. If they reach plus 5 points they win, and if they score minus 5, they lose.

4. Start the players in the tactical situation preceding the one you wish to work on. Upon the coach's signal, which could be a bounce of the ball, the players move into the new positions and play the ball. This practice enables coaches to work on the important transition phase as well as the specified tactical situation.

CHAPTER 5

Individual Tactical Play

In this Chapter, you will learn tips about improving your personal performance in the game situation. Although volleyball is a team game and you must play your part in the team's tactical formations, you also have your own tactical play to consider. You should consider every situation as a battle against an opposing smasher, server, blocker or defender. This is one of the characteristics of volleyball that makes it so appealing to players. As the two teams rotate positions throughout the game, new players are brought into positions where they are challenging each other.

SERVING

The score is 24:23 to your team and it is your serve. No pressure! Serving is the only time in the game when you are in total control. What happens next depends entirely on you. With rally point scoring your serve can win or lose the game for your team. It is not good enough to just walk to the line, throw the ball up and hit it. When you go back to the serving line your team is relying on you to give them a good chance of winning the next rally. Your serve must not only be legal but also put the opponents under pressure.

Of course, you could play safe and just knock the ball into court but that will inevitably give the point to the opposition. Alternatively, you could wind yourself up, throw caution to the wind and go for the ace

serve – a 'win or bust' approach. Neither of these approaches is suited to modern volleyball. You must develop not only an individual serving strategy but also link that in with the overall team strategy developed by your coach.

Fig 126 Serve tough. Remember the advantage lies with the side receiving the ball. There is no point serving a nice easy ball to them. Develop a strong, reliable serve and make life tough for them.

95

Where to Serve

1. Pressure the weak player

If you know one of the opposition is a poor receiver they are a prime target. Play on their particular weakness; playing a particular type of serve, balls that are short or long, that are to a particular side of them. Volleyball is a psychological game, and if you can affect a player's confidence in one part of his/her game then this often puts them off the rest of their game.

2. Disrupt their receive strategy

Teams line up to try to play to their strengths. Do not help them by playing the balls straight at their designated receivers. Try to force other players into playing the ball or the main receiver to move out of position to cover them.

3. Exploit the seam

A ball played between two players forces a decision by both players. If they make it late or get it wrong, you will reap the advantage.

4. Serve deep to disrupt fast attacks

Serve deep if the opposition like to play fast attacks, as this slows the rally down and gives your team more time to watch the movement of players as the ball is passed to the setter.

5. Make life difficult for the setter

When the setter is on one side of the court and intends moving to Position 2, serve down the line. The setter will then lose sight of the ball as he/she moves across court. This can affect their chances of making a good set.

6. Stop them in their tracks

Serve at penetrating setters or groups of players lining up together ready to make a combination attack. This will disrupt their planned movement pattern and force them to simplify their final attack.

7. Hit the substitute but avoid the libero

If a player is substituted onto court do not let them have a chance to settle down – serve at them straight away. They have usually been substituted on to strengthen the team – if you can force them to make an error straight away it will hit team morale. The libero however is their specialist receiver, so keep them out of the game.

8. What happened last time around?

How well was your last serve received? Did the opposition make a successful attack directly from receive? The success level you have been achieving must influence your choice of serve and position.

9. Keep the stars out of the game

Serve away from their best attacker to try to force the setter to play the ball to another smasher. If the ball is received on the opposite side of the court, most setters will turn to face the receiver and then play a forwards set away from their top player.

10. Serve tough

Remember the advantage lies with the side receiving the ball. There is no point serving a nice easy ball to them. Develop a strong, reliable serve and make life tough for them.

Fig 127 Waiting to receive service. Arms well away from the body, eyes on the server, legs bent ready to move into the path of the ball.

RECEIVING SERVICE

As the player receiving the serve, you hold the key to the success of your team's attack. A well-directed and flighted pass from you will give the setter the maximum number of attacking options. As the quality of your pass is reduced so are the attacking options. Your coach can help develop your technique but the application of it in the game situation is up to you.

Master that Pass

1. Are you ready?
Make sure that you are ready to receive the serve. While getting into your receive position keep an eye on the server. Do not be distracted by discussions about the last rally.

2. What happened last time?
Try to remember the characteristics of the serve by the player serving at you. Are all the serves going to the same part of the court? Do not be caught out.

3. Get a clear view
Ensure that you have a clear view of the server, especially if you are in a receive line-up which involves players grouping together.

4. Look at the feet and shoulders
Check the way the server's feet and shoulders are facing, as these usually indicate the direction of the serve.

5. Look at your setter
Make sure you know what route they will take to their setting position and the sets they are offering each attacker.

6. Don't be shy – call for the ball
When the serve reaches its highest point, call for the ball and move to the court position from which you will play the ball. If another player calls, move your position to cover them in case they misplay the ball.

7. Make the angle
You will have to change the angle of the pass towards the setter so try to move yourself into position before you play the ball.

8. Be prepared
Serves can dip and swerve at the last moment so do not assume you have the right court, body and arm position for the contact point. Be ready to make final adjustments.

9. Make eye contact
As you start the pass, focus on the setting point. You must steer the ball mentally as well as physically to the setting point.

10. Help
You are not going to play every serve but you must turn and face the receiver so that if they misplay the ball you are ready to keep the ball in play.

Setter Take Control of the Game!

1. **Set up your team**
   As the setter, your job starts at the end of the previous rally. Move quickly to your position in the receive formation. In some teams you will decide on the line-up that the team will use, and your early positioning will help the rest of the team.

2. **Try to predict where the serve will go**
   Remember the pattern of the serves by each player and look at the position of the server's feet and shoulders, so that you know from where on court to expect the pass.

3. **Check on the match-ups**
   Look at the opposing blockers and determine the strongest attacking position for your team.

4. **Who is going where?**
   Make sure that both you and your attackers are clear about the offence you will run if the pass is good.

5. **Don't delay – be prepared**
   Move into position with your hands up ready to set the ball. Concentrate on deciding where and how to set the ball and not on the actual playing of the ball.

6. **Set the percentage set**
   Set the ball to give your team the best chance of a successful attack and not to a predetermined position regardless of the quality of the pass to you.

7. **React to the flow and tempo of the game**
   At different phases in the game you need to control the game or your team. If an attacker has a bad patch, take the pressure off them for a while and set the ball to another position. When the scores are close in the middle of the game, look to break the opposition's rhythm by introducing a change of pace or point of attack. Near the end of the set when points are critical, go for the in-form or pressure attacker.

8. **Keep your head**
   You have an enormous amount to think about in the game and sometimes you will play the wrong or a less than perfect set and a smasher will be unhappy with you. Do not let it get to you – if you lose your cool or your concentration the game will be over very quickly.

9. **There's another game to play as well**
   In addition to setting you have to play your part in backcourt defence and blocking. Do not leave your defensive position until you are sure another player has covered the ball.

10. **You never stop learning**
    Every rally, every set, every game is a learning experience for you. Reflect on your performance against individuals, teams and passes. One of the greatest assets of top setters is experience.

OPPOSITE ABOVE: *Fig 128 Try to predict where the serve will go. Remember the pattern of the serves by each player and look at the position of the server's feet and shoulders, so that you know from where on court to expect the pass.*

OPPOSITE BELOW: *Fig 129 Use the block. Sometimes the block is sitting in front of you just waiting to roof your smash and push it back in your face. All is not lost however, you can turn the ball either outside or inside and hit hard into the block. If the blocker's hands are not angled inwards, you can gain a deflection off them out of court.*

Ten Ways to Improve Your Hitting

1. **Hit what you are given – Get on with it!**

   Just as the setter has to set the pass he/she has been given, you must attack every set you are given to the best of your ability. Every set is a challenge to your ability and the more you accept that challenge the better you will become. On a bad set get up as fast and high as you can then use the ball, don't lose it. Try to play a shot that interrupts the flow of the game for your opponents, for example, place the ball out of easy reach or make the setter play the ball.

2. **Reach!**

   No matter whether you are 2m or 1.5m tall, you must contact the ball as high as you can. Don't wait for the ball to come down to you; stretch your hitting arm up to raise the contact point and help you go over the block.

3. **Maximize your power**

   The power of your smash depends on a very fast and powerful take-off. A lazy take-off equals a lazy smash. Take off behind the ball and once you are in the air, make sure you keep the line of the smashing action straight and through the shoulder.

4. **Check out the block**

   Look at your blockers – which is the smallest, which is the best, do they get a good line, are they timing their take–off correctly, are the outside blockers' hands angled inwards, do the blockers close the gap with their hands in the air? All these points must be taken into consideration in deciding whether to smash down the line, on the diagonal, or off the block.

5. **Look beyond the block**

   Look at the defensive formation your opponents play. Do they have a player covering behind the block? If so, this will affect where you play the tip or tactical balls. Who is covering the backcourt space left by this defender? There may be a good target for you there. Identify the individual defensive players when you are smashing in each rotational position. Learn to play on their weaknesses – use the tip or tactical smash on slow movers.

6. **Find the gap**

   If the quick hitter has done his/her job and delayed the middle blocker moving to the outside there will be a nice cross-court gap to smash through. If the blockers swing their arms to close the gap, there is a good chance they will deflect the ball and confuse the defence.

7. **Use the block**

   Sometimes the block is sitting in front of you just waiting to roof your smash and push it back in your face. All is not lost however, you can turn the ball either outside or inside and hit hard into the block. If the blocker's hands are not angled inwards you can gain a deflection off them out of court.

8. **Who is the strongest of them all?**

   Sometimes the set is so close to the net there is no way you will be able to hit it past the block. So, get up high, front the ball, use both hands and push against the blockers. The strongest pusher will force the other player back and win the point. A potential defeat turns into a great psychological boost!

9. **The soft touch**

   The ball is set close to the net and you are not close enough to it to push the block off. Play the ball as high onto the block as possible so that they cannot get a firm grip on it. The ball should then come back to your side slowly enough for you to retrieve and counter-attack.

Ten Ways to Improve Your Hitting
continued

10. **And now for something completely different!**
    Do not try to hit the leather off every ball. Keep your opponents guessing by using offspeed smashes and the tip. The tip is a great point winner when it is used on a ball that you are expected to hit and a reliable point saver when every other shot is closed down.

THE SET PASS

As the setter you are in charge of the pattern of play on court. The way you develop that pattern and the way you control the flow of the game will inevitably play a major part in determining the performance level of your team. Training sessions will have honed your ball skills but in the competitive game situation it is your decision-making skills that are most important.

Fig 130 As soon as you realize that one of the other defenders is going to play the ball do not relax and think the job is over. Move into a position where you can play the ball if the defender either misplays it or is forced to just try to keep it in the air.

Ten Tips to Improve Your Blocking Statistics

1. **Get those hands up**
   Do not waste valuable above-the-net blocking time. As soon as you leave the ground, your hands should be in the blocking zone. While you are waiting to block, get those hands up as a warning to the attacker that you are there. The bigger the net area that you occupy the less they can see of your server!

2. **Who are the attackers and where are they?**
   You cannot afford to wait until the smashers approach the net to see who they are. Identify their shirt numbers, location and role, for example, No. 6 Quick hitter in front left and call them out for your teammates.

3. **Be nosey – listen in**
   Listen to the opposition, watch to see if you can identify signals to and from the setter or hear their instructions. Remember which moves or shots players like to make so you are able to anticipate them.

4. **Position yourself according to the situation**
   Do not just stand at the net and wait. Look at the match ups and get into position to block them, for example, if the frontcourt player is setting then his/her blocker should move nearer the centre.

5. **Keep your eyes open**
   Remember the smasher has control of the situation until he/she hits the ball. You must keep watching his/her movements as well as the ball. This way you can cover the tip or the attempt to play off the block.

6. **Work it out**
   If the smasher passes you, do not get dispirited. Try to retain a mental picture of the blocking action so that next time you block the same situation you can make the necessary adjustments to your positioning or timing. Most good teams can only expect to win points from four or five blocks a set, but in many cases you can force your opponents to hit out or directly to a defender.

7. **Maximize your width**
   You want to cover the largest net area you can so spread your fingers wide and rotate your wrists outwards. Compared with keeping your fingers together and hands vertical this can increase your coverage by 50 per cent.

8. **Don't lean**
   If you are caught out of position and cannot get right across to the smasher do not swing your arms across to try to close the gap. This will give them a chance to play off your hands. Block vertically and penetrate the net. You will still cover part of the net area and may be lucky if they cut the ball inside. Your defenders will have a better view and chance to defend.

9. **Don't be pushed off the ball**
   If the setter puts the ball on top of the net, you must be prepared for a tussle with the attacker. Spread your fingers wide. Penetrate the net as far as you can, lock the arms at the elbows and be prepared to push hard as the smasher touches the ball. There is a little matter of pride here – make sure they are the ones pushed off the ball!

10. **Don't just stand there**
    If you are too late to block, do not give up, but move back from the net to cover behind the block for the short balls. This will allow the remaining backcourt players to stay back for the smash.

SMASHING

The French have a name for the smasher who puts brawn before brains – 'spiker bestial'! This sums up the sort of player who typically remembers the one brilliant smash and forgets the ten others in the net, block or out of court. Think before you smash must be your motto.

BLOCKING

The smasher always has the advantage against the blocker and it is very satisfying when you, as a blocker, are able to win the rally. However, success in blocking comes as much from good reading of the game and good preparation as from excellent technique.

BACKCOURT DEFENCE

There is tremendous satisfaction in successfully receiving a smash or anticipating the tip and tactical ball, often more than in actually smashing the ball. However, individual defence is mentally as well as physically exhausting.

If a player chases off court after the ball do not just watch, move to a position halfway between him/her and the net, so that you can help. Let the player know you are in support so that he/she will not have to try and retrieve the ball as well as play it back over the net.

Volleyball is a team game played by individuals. There is a personal responsibility to produce the highest level of play especially when things are not going well for the team or some of the other players. It is essential that you maintain this dual focus of maximizing your individual performance and integrating those efforts with the rest of the team's.

Ten Ways to Improve Your Defence

1. **No time to rest!**
   The first thing to remember when you rotate into the back row is that it is not a pause between bouts of smashing but an essential part of the game. A good defender will never stop working mentally or physically.

2. **You need an attitude problem**
   Nothing is going to get between you and floor! You can really upset attackers if you get their best shot up. Be positive from the start; every ball is coming to you and you will not be beaten.

3. **Your base is only a starting point**
   Your defensive system will give you a starting base that you should occupy as soon as the ball is in the other half of the court. As soon as they pass the ball to their setter, you must adjust your position.

4. **Read and react**
   If the ball is set back from the net, it will be hit deeper into the backcourt if it is to pass over the block. A set near to the net will land in the middle of the court. Move forwards or backwards along the anticipated direction line of the smash according to the set. Line up with the feet and hips of the smasher, as most will hit along the power line – the way they are facing. If the block is going to be well-formed move so you can see what is happening. If it will be late or incomplete, expect the ball to come through the gap.

5. **Get square to the smash**
   Position yourself so that your hips and shoulders are square to the smash. This will stop the ball bouncing off your arms out of court.

Ten Ways to Improve Your Defence
continued

6. **Watch the smasher's arm**
   Try to see if he/she intends to play a tip or tactical ball. In these instances his/her arm will slow down and straighten just before contact.

7. **Keep your weight forwards**
   In the defensive position you need to be able to move forwards quickly to play the ball. Once the ball is hit you have no time to initiate movement so your body weight needs to be ahead of your toes so that you can move into the ball if needed.

8. **React to the smash**
   As the ball is contacted move to place yourself between it and the floor. This should be an almost instantaneous reaction to the hit.

   Try to play the ball within your base of support and angle your hips towards the setting zone.

9. **Two arms are better than one**
   Always aim to play the ball using both arms. Not only does this increase the area of contact with the ball, it is stronger, thus preventing the force of the ball knocking one arm out of the way.

10. **Help**
    As soon as you realize that one of the other defenders is going to play the ball do not relax and think the job is over. Move into a position where you can play the ball if the defender either misplays it or is forced to just try to keep it in the air.

CHAPTER 6

Coaching

In some team games it has not been the custom to have a coach, but, from the early days, it has been recognized that it is essential to have coaches in volleyball. Apart from the fact that the players must each learn a range of techniques, the tactics in the game situation require someone to observe them and make any necessary adjustments.

> **The Role of the Coach**
>
> The role of the coach is to help players play to the best of their abilities, not to use them to gain success for himself.

The volleyball coach has duties before, during and after the game.

COACH'S DUTIES

Pre-Match

1. Taking and preparing the training sessions.
2. Planning the team tactical systems.
3. Analysing the opposition and preparing the tactics needed to beat them.

Match

1. Organizing the warm-up.
2. Choosing the starting six players and their rotational positions. This must be handed to the scorer along with the names and numbers of all team players before the start of the first set.
3. At the start of each subsequent set, handing the team rotation list to the second official.
4. Calling time-outs and substitutions as required and permitted.
5. Analysing the team's performance during the game and making any changes in line-up, tactics or players that are necessary.
6. Controlling the behaviour of players on and off the bench.

Post-Match

1. Ensuring that the team cheers the opposition and shakes hands no matter what the result.
2. With the team captain, thanking the two officials and scorers for their work.
3. Reviewing the performance of the team and your own coaching during the game with a view to planning future training sessions.

SEASONAL TRAINING

It is essential that you have a clear idea of what you are trying to achieve with your team. You should have a seasonal plan for team development. This plan should divide the year as follows: technical and physical preparation, tactical and game preparation, competition period and warm-down and break.

Technical and Physical Preparation

Once the competitive season is under way it is difficult for the coach to start developing new techniques with players or even correcting major faults. The couple of months between competitive seasons is the time when the coach can concentrate on technique perfection and development. At the same time, players can be undertaking major strength building training programmes. During this period the coach must build the foundations on which the team's tactical performance is to be structured.

Tactical and Game Preparation

This period will last about a month for most teams. During it, the coach will be spending most of the time making the tactical systems he/she wants to employ during the coming season work effectively. Pre-season tournaments will be particularly useful for seeing how these are operating in the game situation.

The Competitive Season

By the start of the season the players' physical, technical and tactical preparation should be approaching their peak. The problem for the coach is to maintain this high level throughout the competition period, which may last six months or more. It is unlikely that every player will be able to maintain form, and at times the whole team performance will suffer as a result.

The skill in coaching is being able to identify the cause of the problem as early as possible and adjust the training programme accordingly. Training sessions should not have a particularly high level of physical work as the emphasis must be on preparation for the demands of the next match, particularly in relation to individual and team tactics. Most leagues do have a few weeks' break during the

middle that the coach will be able to use to work on any significant changes in team tactics that have been shown to be needed.

The Warm-Down and Break

At the end of the season, players will be feeling mentally and physically jaded, and the coach should gradually decrease the training load. It is a good idea to attend some of the large outdoor tournaments where although matches are competitive, they are played in a much more relaxed spirit. There should then be a break of four to six weeks before the next season' s cycle begins.

THE TRAINING SESSION

The individual training session should be structured, and not just a motley collection of a few drills plus a game. Each session should ideally consist of the following sections:

1. Warm-up exercises to avoid muscular injuries.
2. Technical exercises related to the main theme of the session.
3. Concentrated work on the technical or tactical theme of the session.
4. Controlled game situation emphasizing the technical and tactical work.
5. Warm-down exercises to avoid stiffness.

The coach should try to cut down to a minimum the breaks in the practical sessions while points are explained to players, as this will lead to some players losing their concentration. If there are points that need to be said to particular players and not the whole group, these players should be taken out of the exercises while discussion or explanation takes place. Training drills should be linked together to avoid wasting time by starting in different places and groups. There are hundreds of drills which can be used and coaches should build up their own manual of drills that they find are useful, including ones they have developed themselves.

ANALYSING THE OPPOSITION

The opportunity should always be taken to scout the opposition and build up a dossier about their tactical systems – for example, the strengths and weaknesses of individual players, and results of previous matches between the teams.

Look at the formations used for receive of service and the rotational order the team usually plays its players. Try to match this with your own team so that your best receivers are opposite their best servers and vice versa. Look at their defensive system and their blockers. Place your best line smasher against their weakest or smallest line blocker and so on.

Identify individual players who are weak at receiving the service or smash, those who are not fast or mobile enough to cover the tip or tactical ball, and get your players to exploit these weaknesses.

It is a coach's job to see that his/her players go into a game knowing what they are up against and how to deal with the situation.

MATCH DUTIES

The rules require the coach to give the scorer before the match a list of all players, any licences they need and their shirt numbers. All shirts must be numbered back and front between one and eighteen.

The coach and captain must also sign the score sheet to signify that the list recorded is correct. The coach must also complete a rotation slip that shows the order in which his/her

first six players will line up on court and the shirt numbers of each player in that position. The second official will use this to check during the game that the correct positions are being maintained. At the start of each new set, a new slip must be completed (Fig 131).

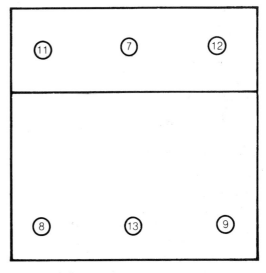

Fig 131 The rotation slip that must be filled in before each set and handed to the second official. It shows the players' shirt numbers and court positions at the start of each set.

The warm-up should start around thirty minutes before the scheduled match is due to begin. It will include a general warm-up without the ball, work in pairs smashing and digging to each other, and then smashing over the net. The second official is responsible for timing the length of smashing over the net and seeing that teams change from smashing at Position 4 to smashing at Position 2. Usually a short period is also allowed for teams to practise serving.

The starting six players should line up on the baseline until the referee calls them onto court. All the other players and the coach will be on the team bench or keeping warm at the end of the court just to the side.

The coach may coach from the side of the court provided he/she stays between the attack line and the baseline without interfering with play. In each set, coaches may request two time-outs, each of 30sec duration, to talk to the teams. These periods should be used carefully to ensure that what is said is useful and will improve the team's performance.

Substitutions may be called by asking the second official at the end of the rally. The player going on must be ready with tracksuit off, standing by the scorer's table. The second official will make the two players who are changing wait by the sideline until the scorer has recorded their numbers. Any of the starting six players may be replaced once by a player off court in each set. If the coach wishes to put the original player back on court, he/she may only be substituted back on, during that set, for the replacement player. Each time a player on court comes off counts as one substitution and a maximum of six substitutions are allowed in each set. Substitutions are used to replace players who have momentarily lost form or because the coach wishes to introduce an additional attacker in the front row, a defender in the back or a new setter.

The 'libero' player may go on and off court in between rallies without consulting the second official and these exchanges do not count as part of a team's six substitutions.

The coach should watch both teams on court, so that information about the opposition's tactics can be passed to players and tactics altered if necessary. The coach is as active during the match as the players.

It is very helpful if an assistant coach, or reserve player sits by the coach and undertakes an analysis of the match. This can be used not only to record details of the teams' performance in selected areas, but also to build up a bank of information about the opposition that will form the basis of a future game plan.

POST-MATCH DUTIES

Volleyball has a tremendous reputation as a very sporting game. The fact that the two teams do not have any physical contact during the game contributes to this, as does the fact that traditionally players will admit to touching the net or ball when the referee has not seen the touch.

The coach has a responsibility to control players' behaviour on the court, on the bench and after the game. Dissent, abuse or any other form of unsportsmanlike behaviour should result in discipline from the coach before the referee is forced to act officially.

At the end of the game it is pleasing to see in volleyball that the players always shake hands with each other and give the opposition a cheer. Coaches and captains as a matter of courtesy always thank the match officials and their respective counterparts after the game.

Although self-discipline by the players is important, the coach is ultimately responsible for making sure that the players continue volleyball's sporting traditions.

The final duty of the coach after the game, often done twenty-four hours later, is to review the match from not only a playing but also a coaching point of view. It is very good coaching to arrange for players to turn up half an hour early at the next training session so that they can discuss with the coach the way they played and what changes need to be made.

Glossary

Attack Line A line in each half drawn across the width of the court parallel to the net 3m from centreline.

Attack Zone The area between the attack line and the centreline. A backcourt player may not direct the ball from within the attack zone into the opponents' court, unless the ball is below net height when struck. If the player takes off behind the attack line, he/she may hit the ball in any way and at any height before he/she lands in the attack area.

Backcourt Player Players in Positions 1, 6 or 5 at the time of service.

Block The block is the counter to the smash. The opposing players jump up and place a wall of hands in the path of the smashed ball with the intention of blocking its path across the net. Only frontcourt players may block.

Combination Attack Two or more players will approach the net at approximately the same time. The opposing blockers will not be sure which of the players will make the attack, what kind of attack it will be and from what position in court.

Covering the Smash When a player is smashing the ball his/her team-mates come closer to him/her in case the block sends the ball back into their court. They will then be in position to play the ball before it touches the ground.

Dig or Bump Pass The ball is played on the outstretched forearms. This pass is used when the ball is travelling fast or very low.

Double Foul Players on opposite sides of the net simultaneously commit faults. The referee orders the point to be replayed.

Double Touch One player touches the ball twice in succession or the ball touches two parts of his/her body at different times.

First Official The chief official in the game. He sits at the side of the court so that he/she looks along the top of the net.

First Pass The pass made, on receive of the serve or smash, to the setter.

Floating Service The ball is hit in such a way that the serve moves through the air without any spin, thus giving it the appearance of floating in the air. The serve can dip or swerve suddenly when the speed drops.

Forearm Pass The ball is played on the inside of the outstretched forearms. Usually used to play the served ball.

Frontcourt Player One of the players in Position 4, 3 or 2 at the time of service.

Held Ball A ball that is held simultaneously by two players above the net during the blocking action. The point is replayed.

Libero Player This player may be substituted into the three backcourt positions and acts as a specialist defender. He/she may not serve, act as a setter or play in the frontcourt. Substitutions of the libero do not count as one of the team's six allowable substitutions in a set.

Match The best of three or five sets.

Penetration The practice of bringing a backcourt setter into the frontcourt to set. This means that the frontcourt setter can act as a third smasher.

Play Set Hitter In a combination attack the Play Set Hitter plays the second tempo shot. Most often this is the attacker playing in Position 2.

Quick Hitter Normally the central attacker in the frontcourt who specializes in hitting balls set close to the setter and low above the net.

Rally The complete unit of play from the service until play is stopped by the referee and a point is awarded.

Recovery Dive A technique used to play balls well in front or to the side of players. By diving towards the ball and playing it on the back of the hand before landing, the point is saved.

Release Hitter The player who hits a high set on the outside of the court in position 4. When there is a combination attack the Release Hitter is the safety shot.

Rotation On regaining service, teams rotate one position clockwise so that a new player comes to the serving position.

Second Official He stands opposite the referee and moves up and down the sidelines on his/her side of the court.

Service Area A 3m-wide channel of indefinite length is formed by the extension of the right sideline and the serving line, which is marked 3m from this sideline. The server must be in this area when he/she contacts the ball.

Set Pass This is the volley pass, which is played near to and above the net for the smasher to hit.

Setter The player whose job it is to play the set pass. A specialist player is normally used because the job is demanding and requires a high level of skill.

Shoot Set Sometimes known as the parallel set. It is played fast and low across the court for the smasher to hit. When timed effectively it results in a very fast attack.

Short or Quick Set A set played near to the setter and only a short distance above the net. This also is a very fast method of attacking.

Smasher The player whose job it is to complete the attack by hitting the ball across the net.

Substitution Six players are on court at a time and a team may have a further six players off court. These players can be changed by substitution when the ball is dead. A maximum of six substitutions may be made in each set by each team.

Swing Hitter This outside hitter starts his/her approach from a position near the centre of the court moving towards the outside of the court. This in–out movement pattern hides him/her from the frontcourt blockers and means that the blockers have to change from their normal movement pattern.

Switching The technique of changing the positions of players during the rally so that a more effective line-up is obtained.

Time-out Each team may halt play in any set for two periods of 30sec each. Time-outs are used by the coach to give his/her team advice.

Tip Instead of smashing the ball, the attacker plays the ball with his/her fingertips just over or to the side of the block.

Volley Pass The ball is played on the fingers of both hands simultaneously in such a way that it does not come to rest.

Index